First Contact

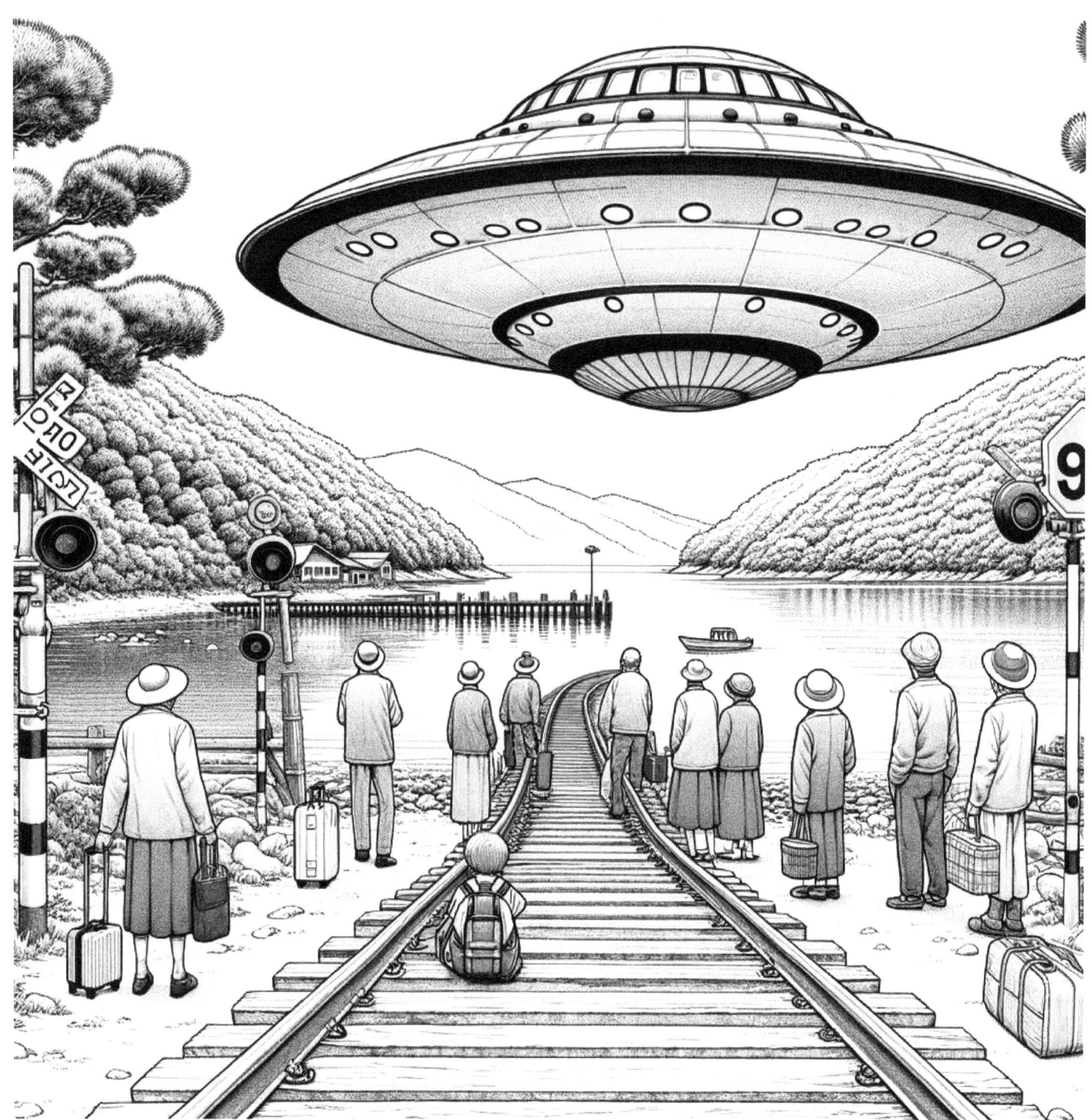

Figure 1. First contact...a small town near the coast in Wakayama

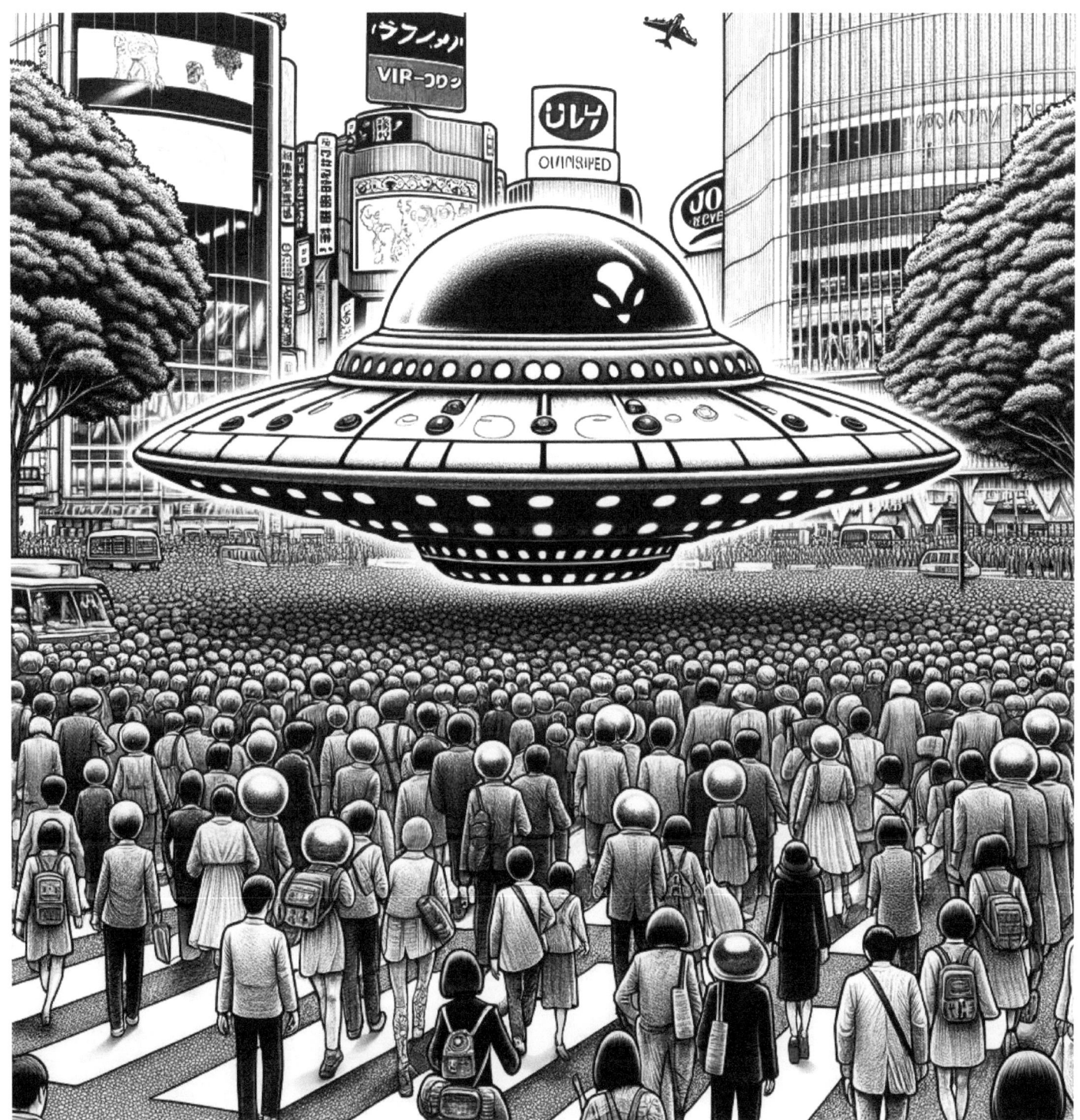

Figure 2. Tokyo madness...and assimilation

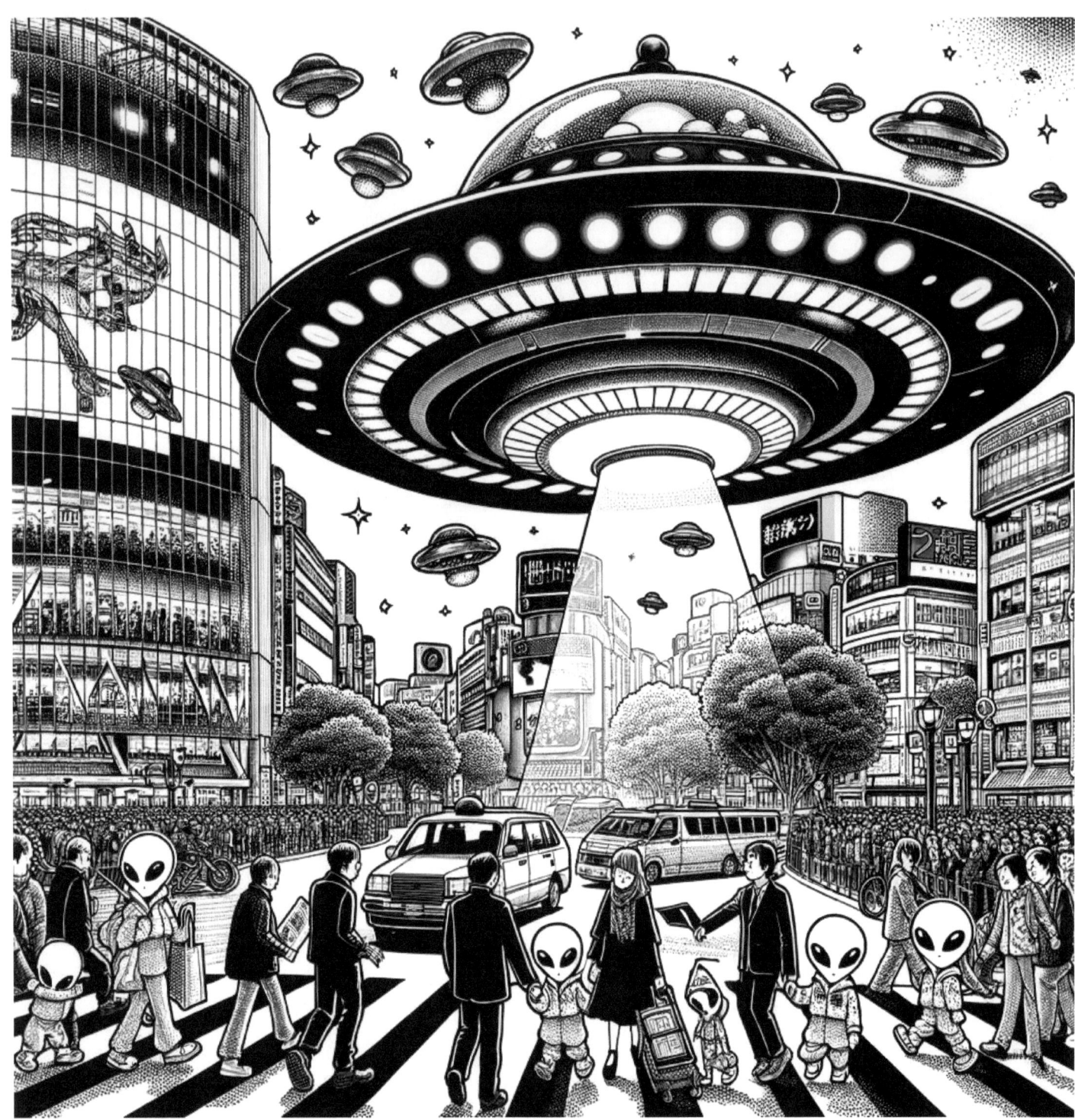

Figure 3. Assimilation complete

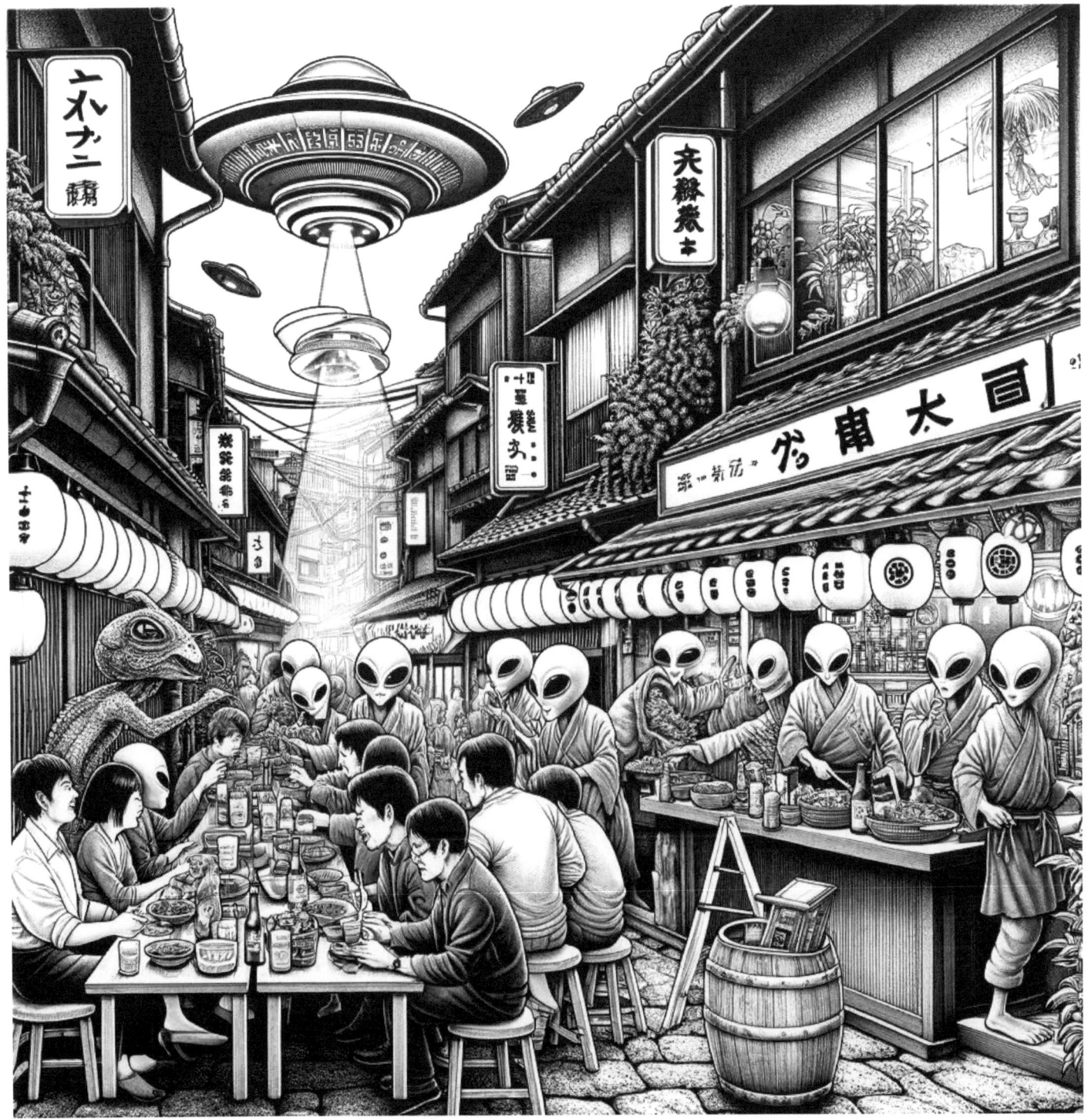

Figure 4. Friday afternoon...enjoying the local izakaya bar with the pals

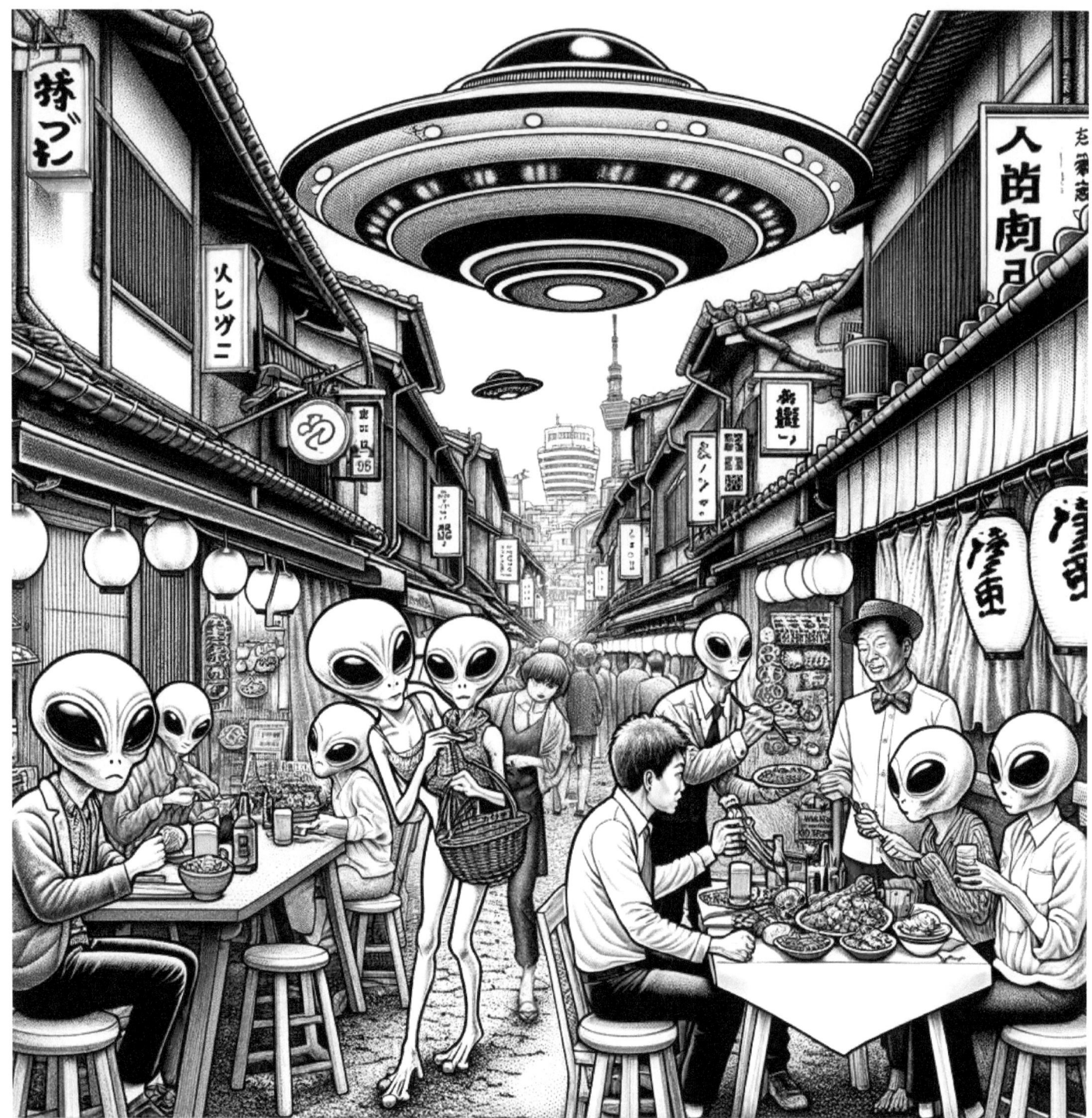

Figure 5. Weekend out with the family

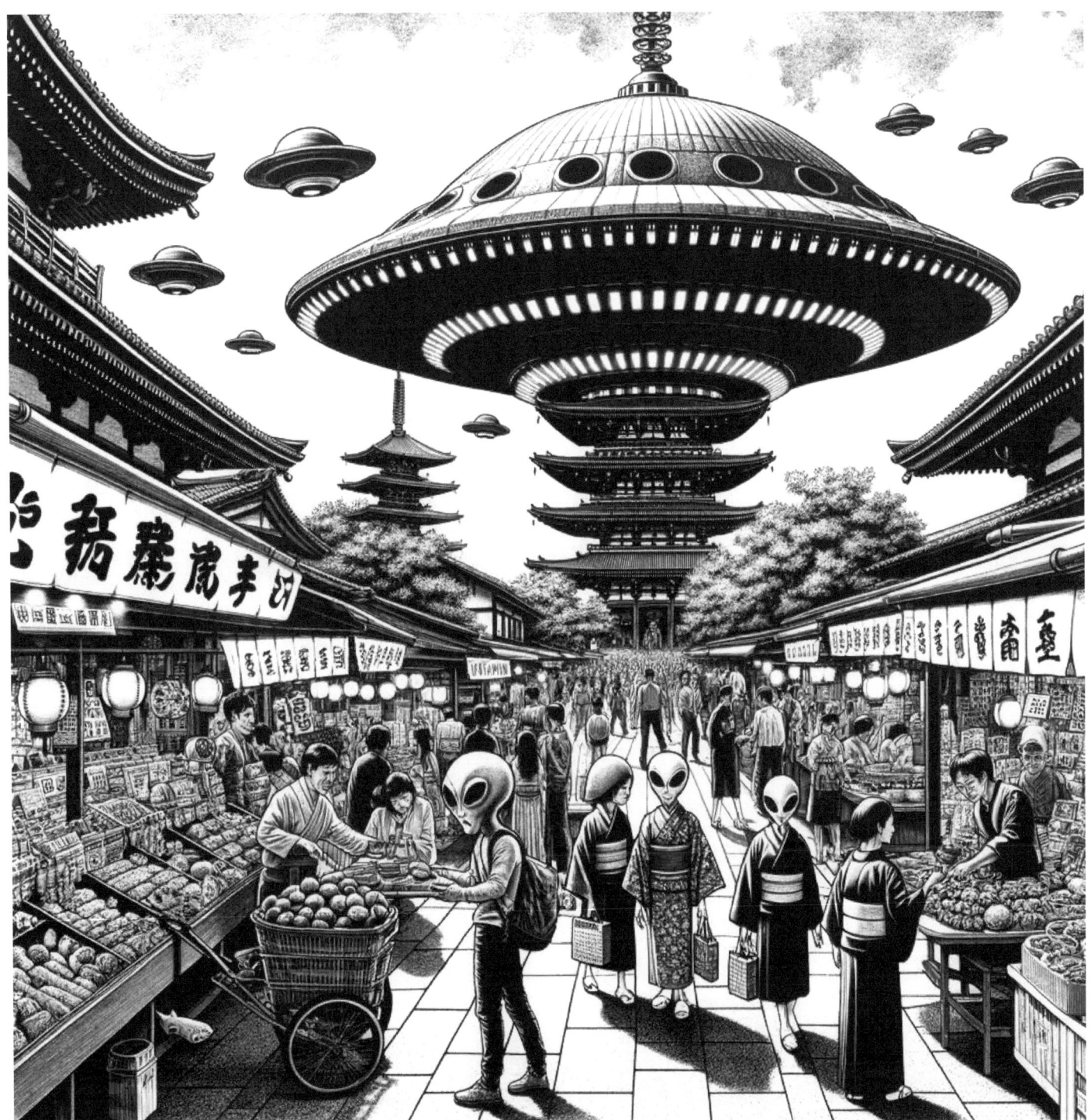

Figure 6. Absorbing...the rich culture and sights

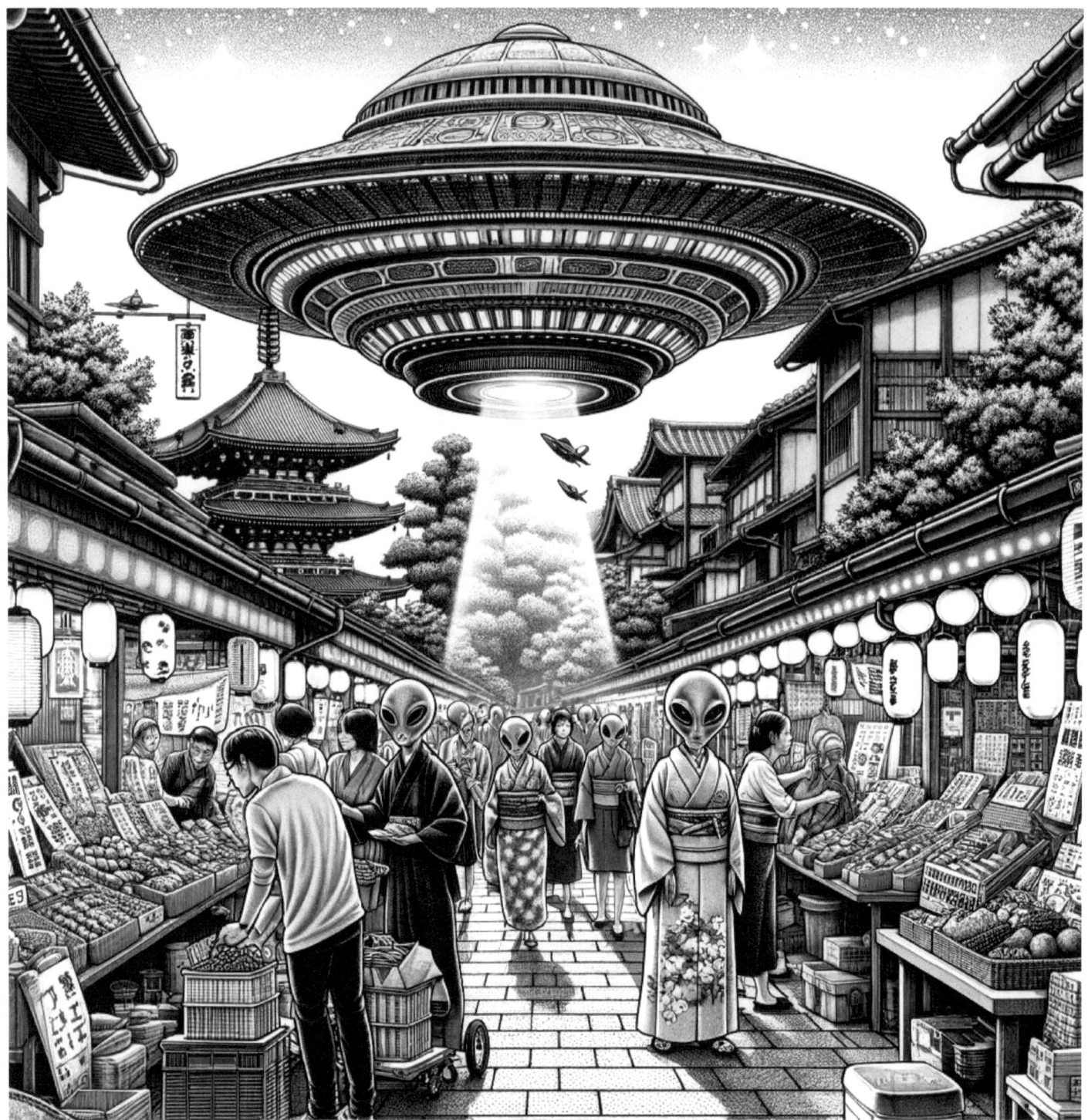

Figure 7. Kimono time in Kyoto

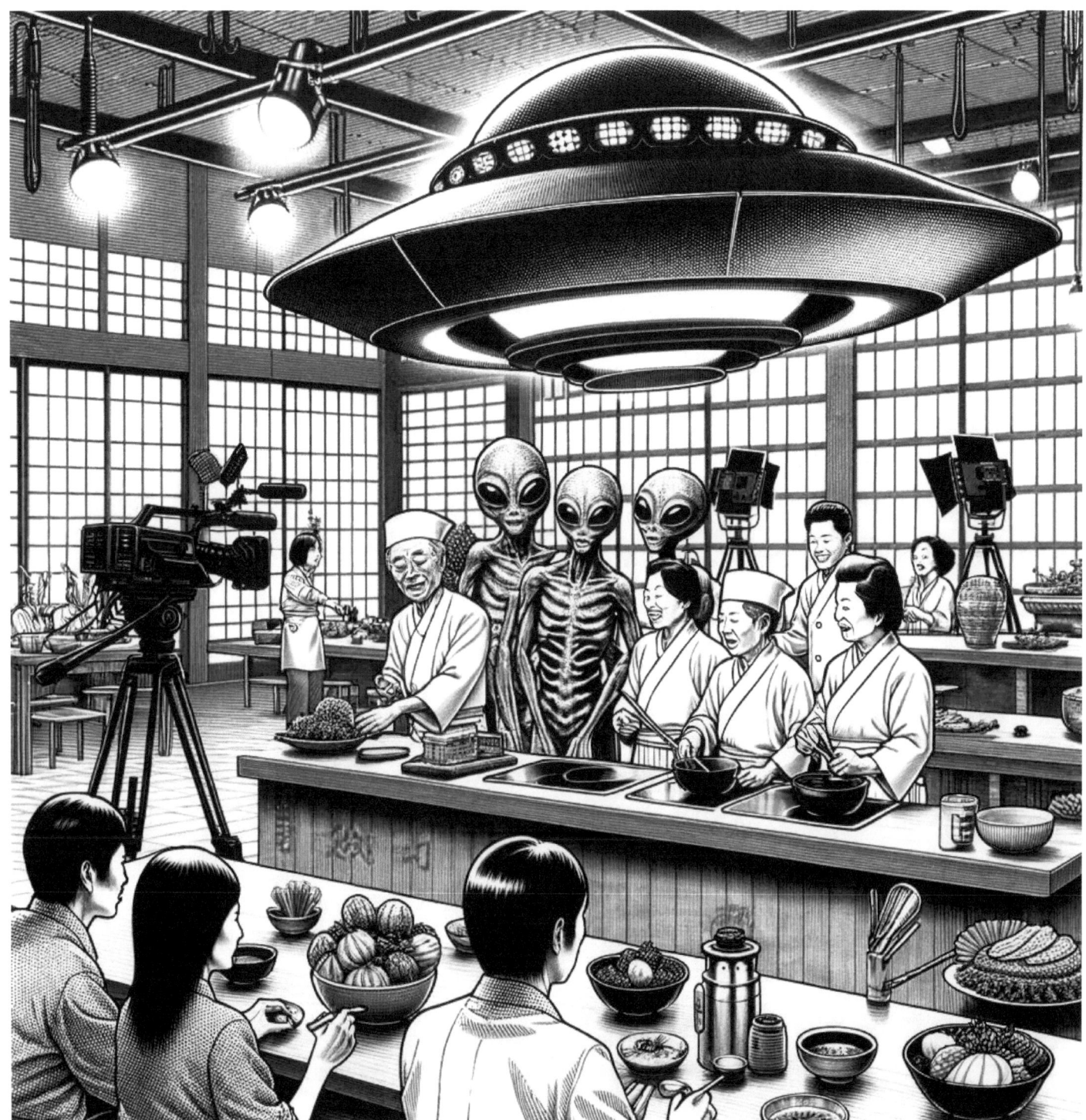

Figure 8. Food show celebrities

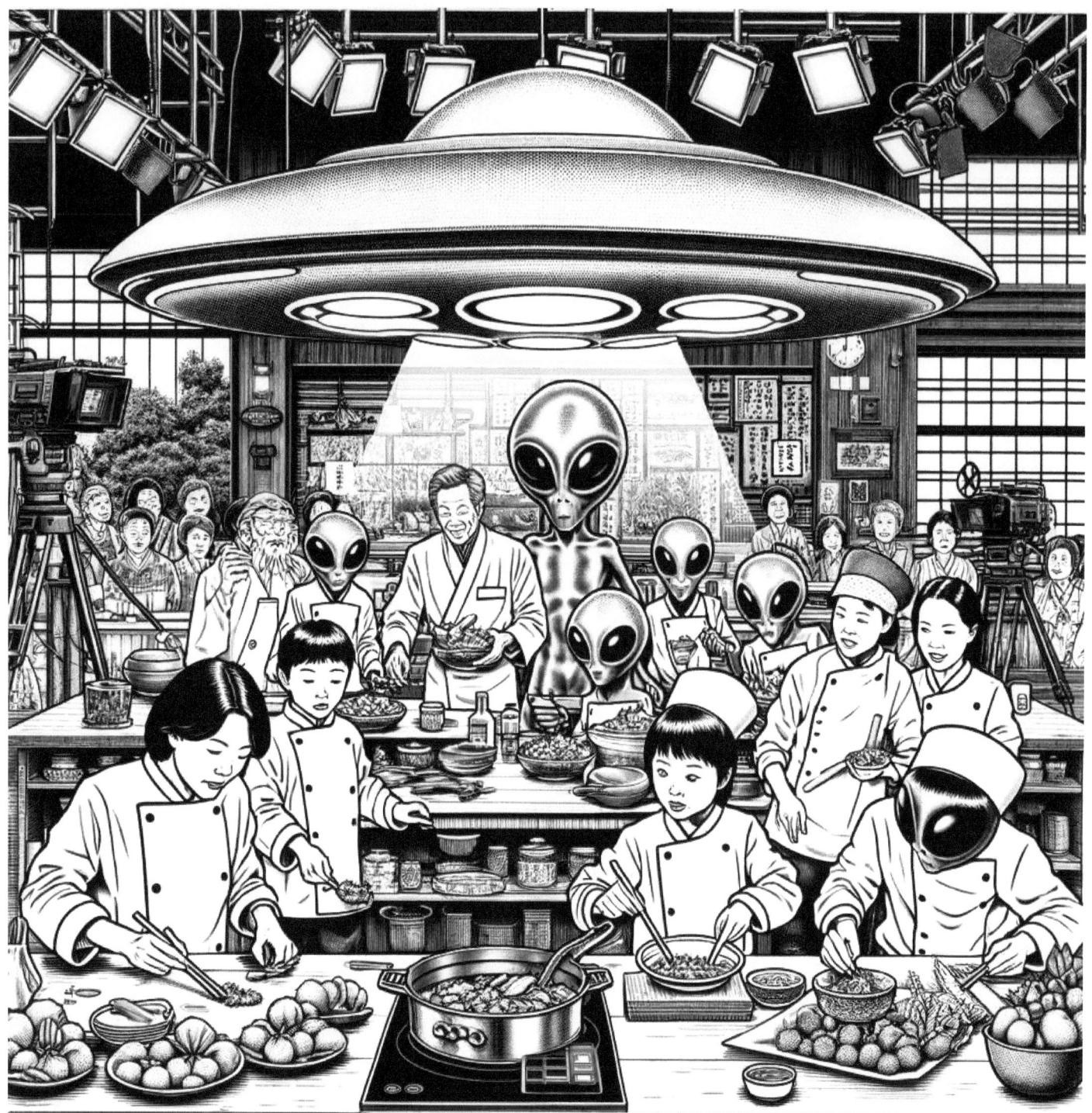

Figure 9. Iron Chef

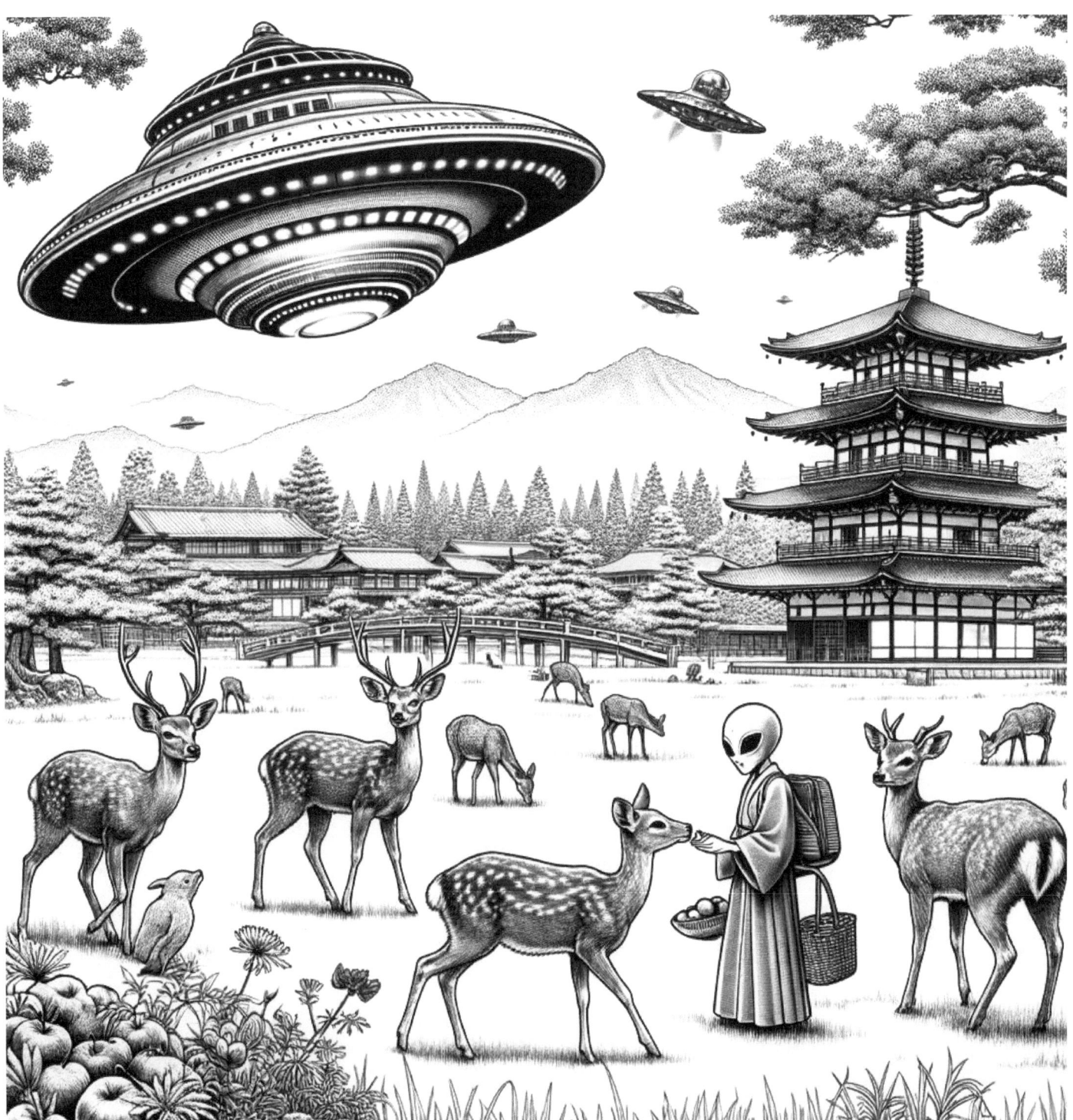

Figure 10. Unwinding with the deer in Nara

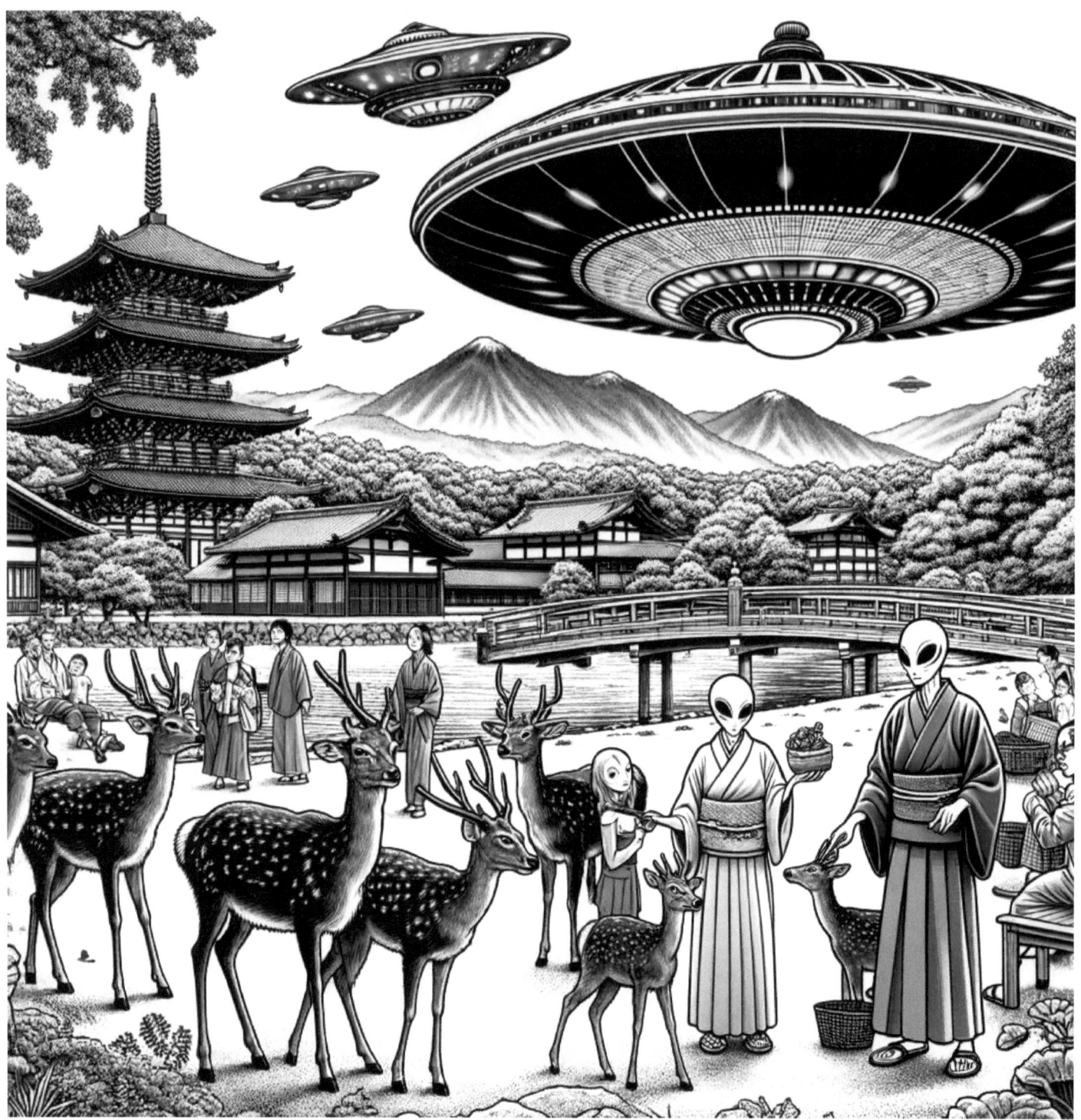

Figure 11. Ah...Japan is so peaceful

Dinos and Tentacles!

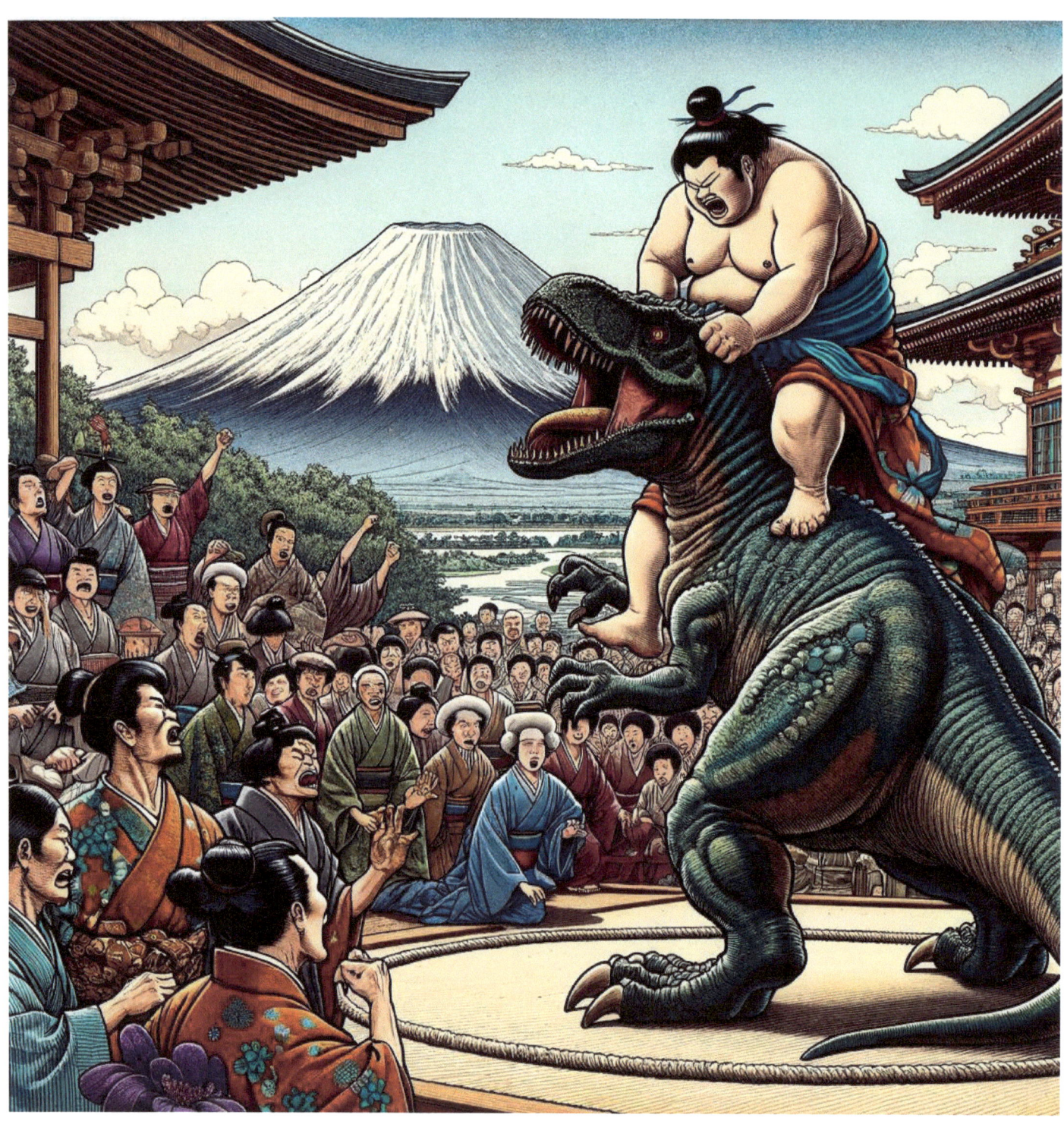

Figure 12. Who will be the first ever Yokozuna champion of Japan? A life or death match...

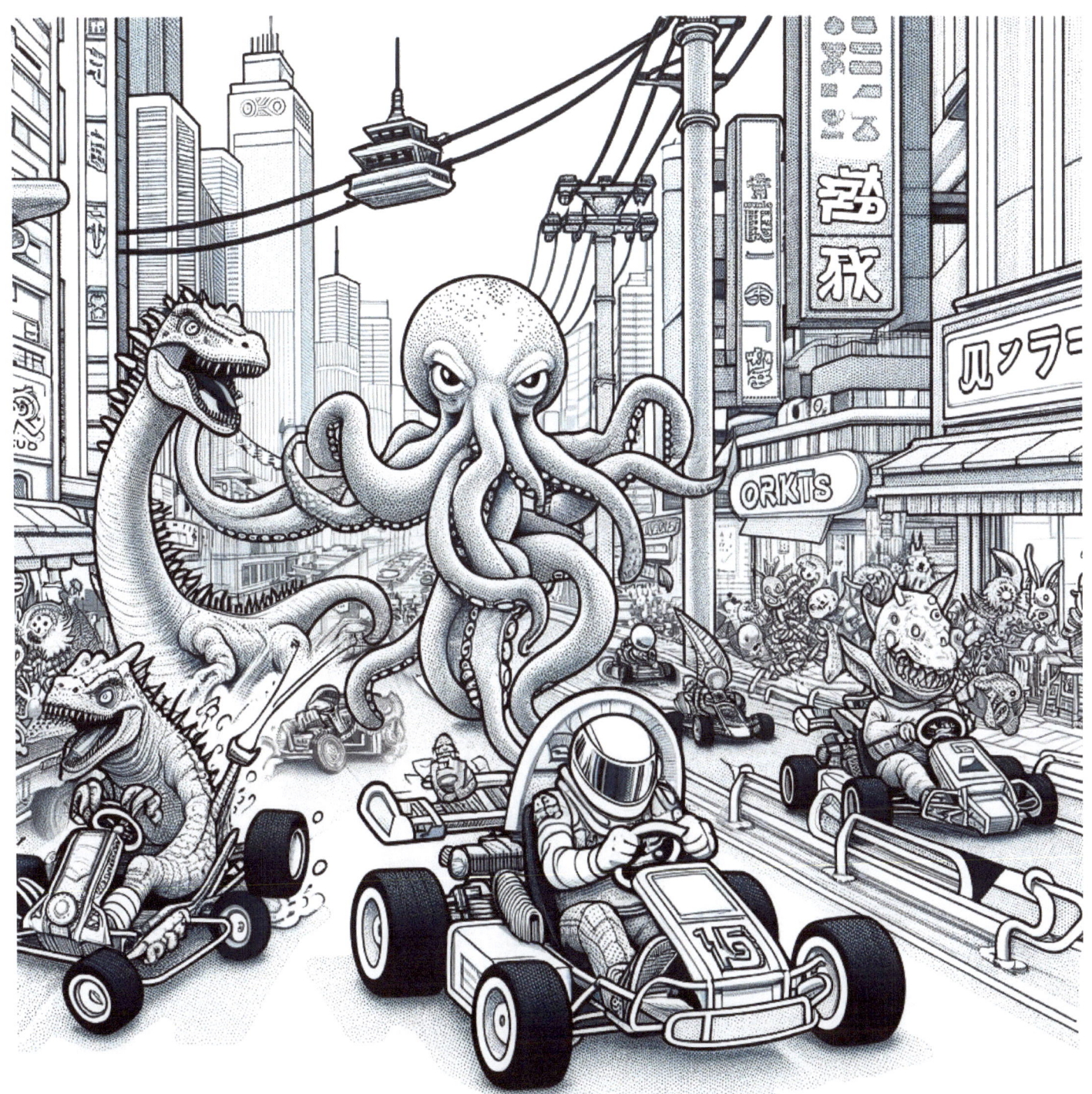

Figure 13. Super mar... madness kart, Tokyo edition...and that giant iguana's about to crash

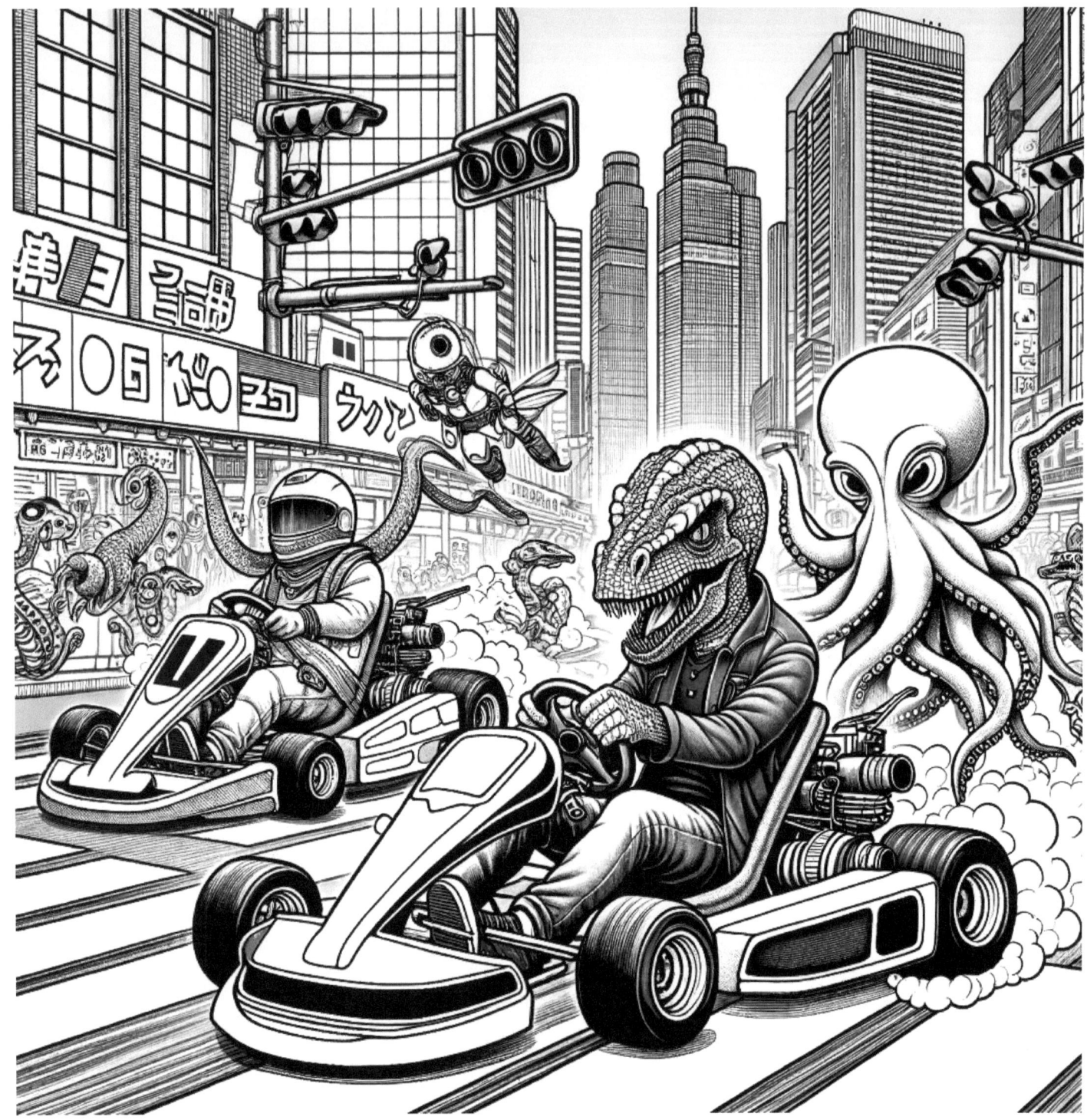

Figure 14. Almost to the finish line...dang that octopus is pretty fast! Well, he has way more than eight legs...

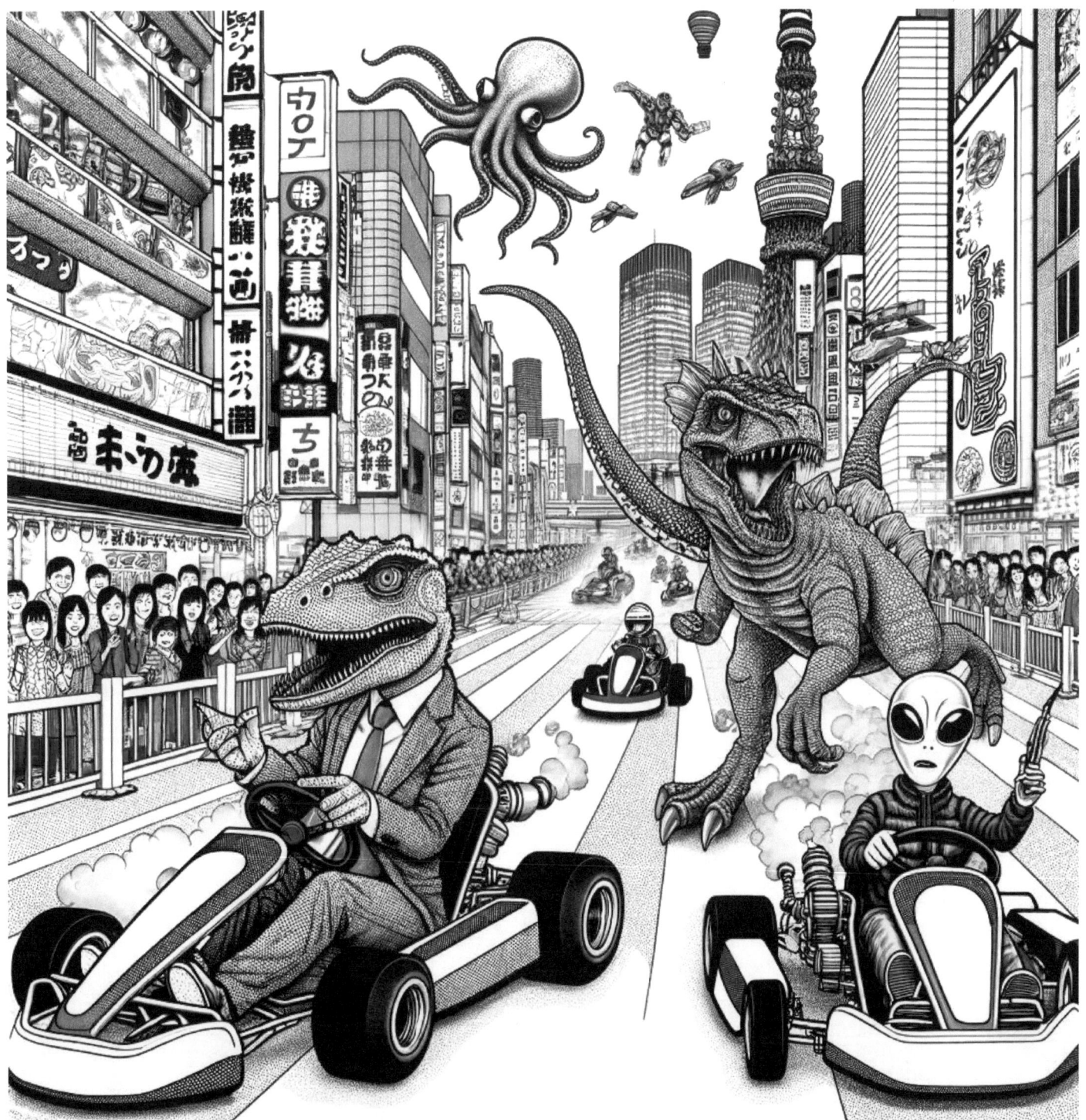

Figure 15. Tokyo rush hour…hey bud, don't you have a flying saucer?

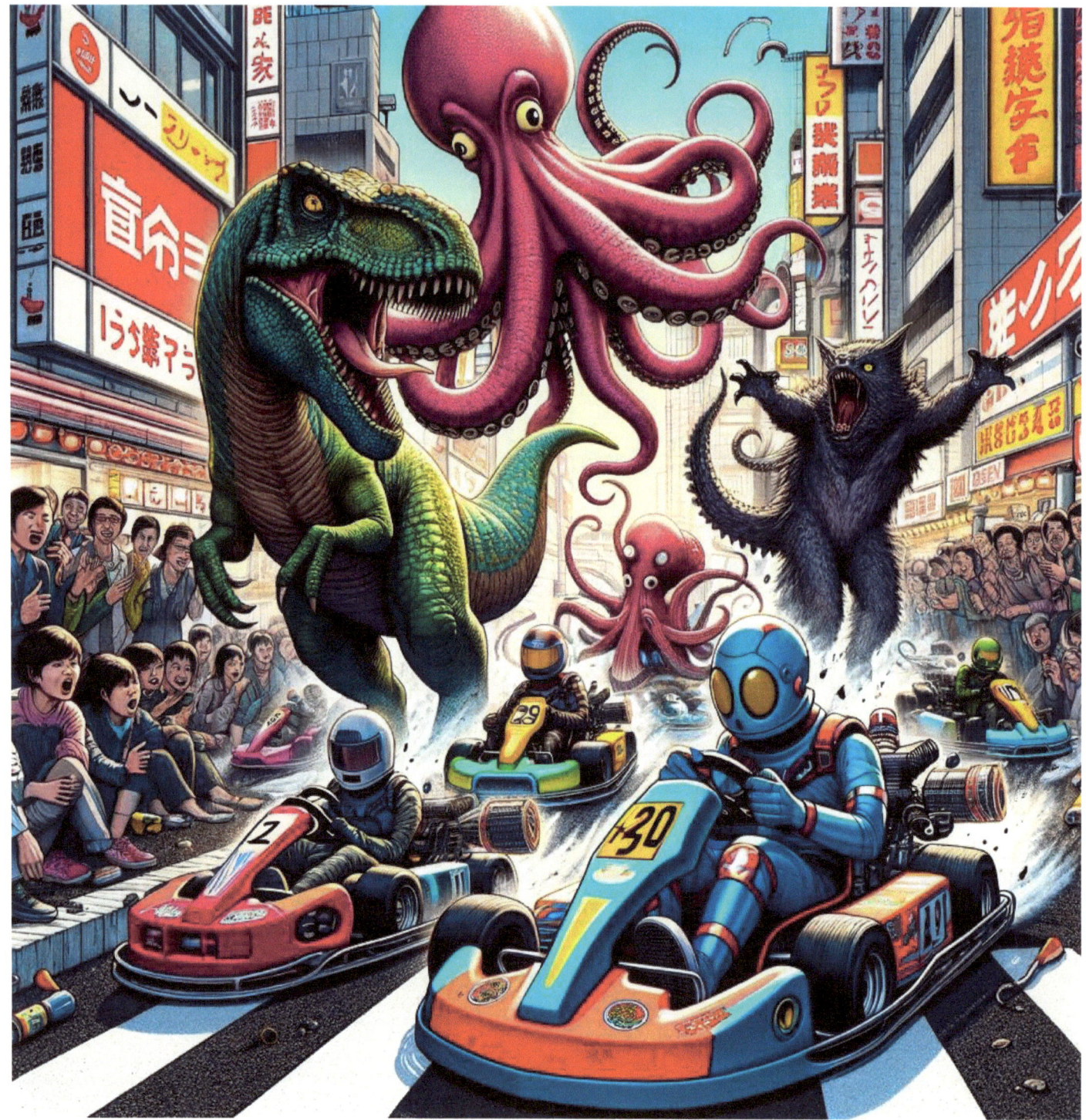

Figure 16. Hey, looks like a video game cover art from the early 90's!

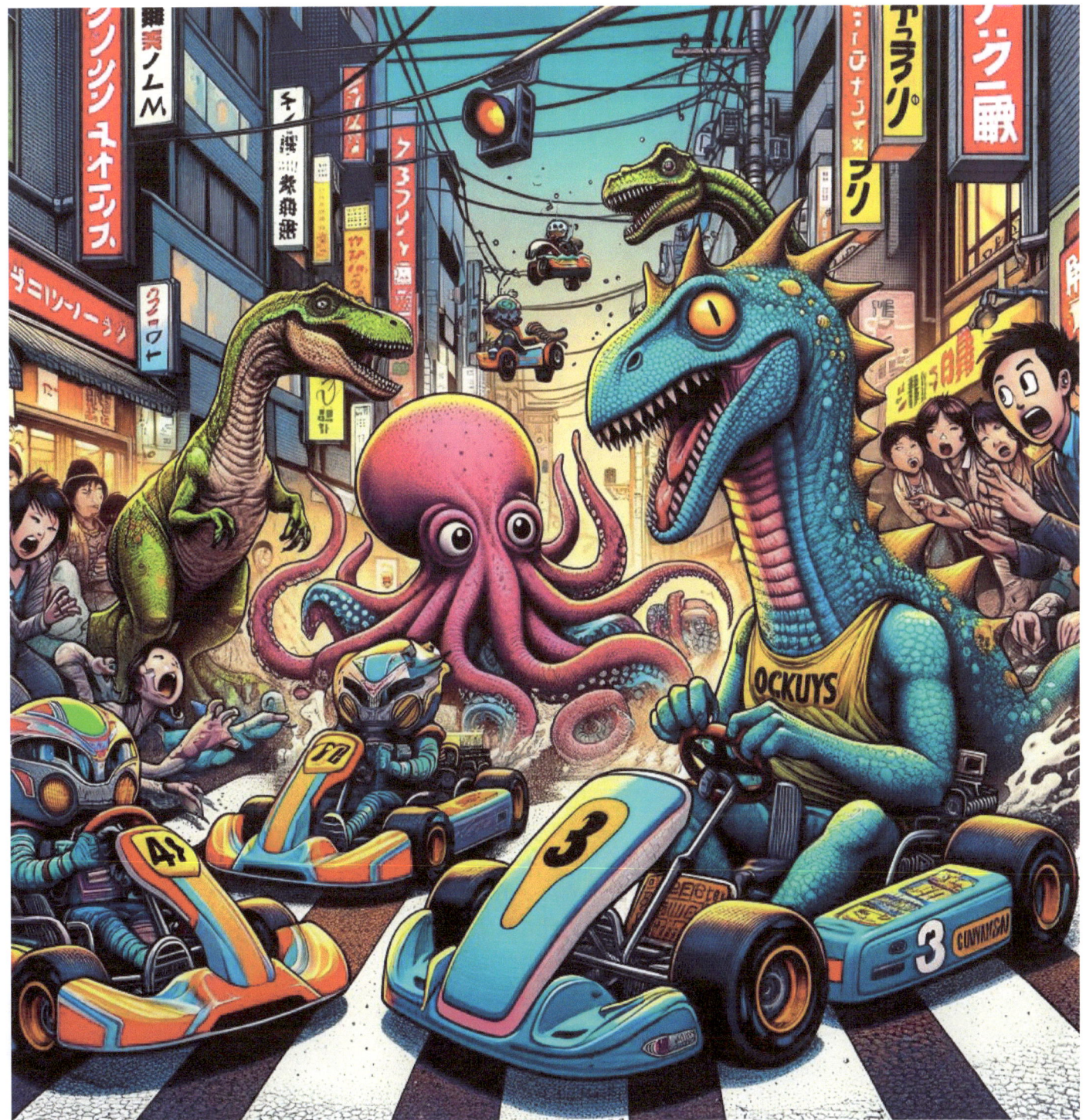

Figure 17. The younger generation training in the backstreets

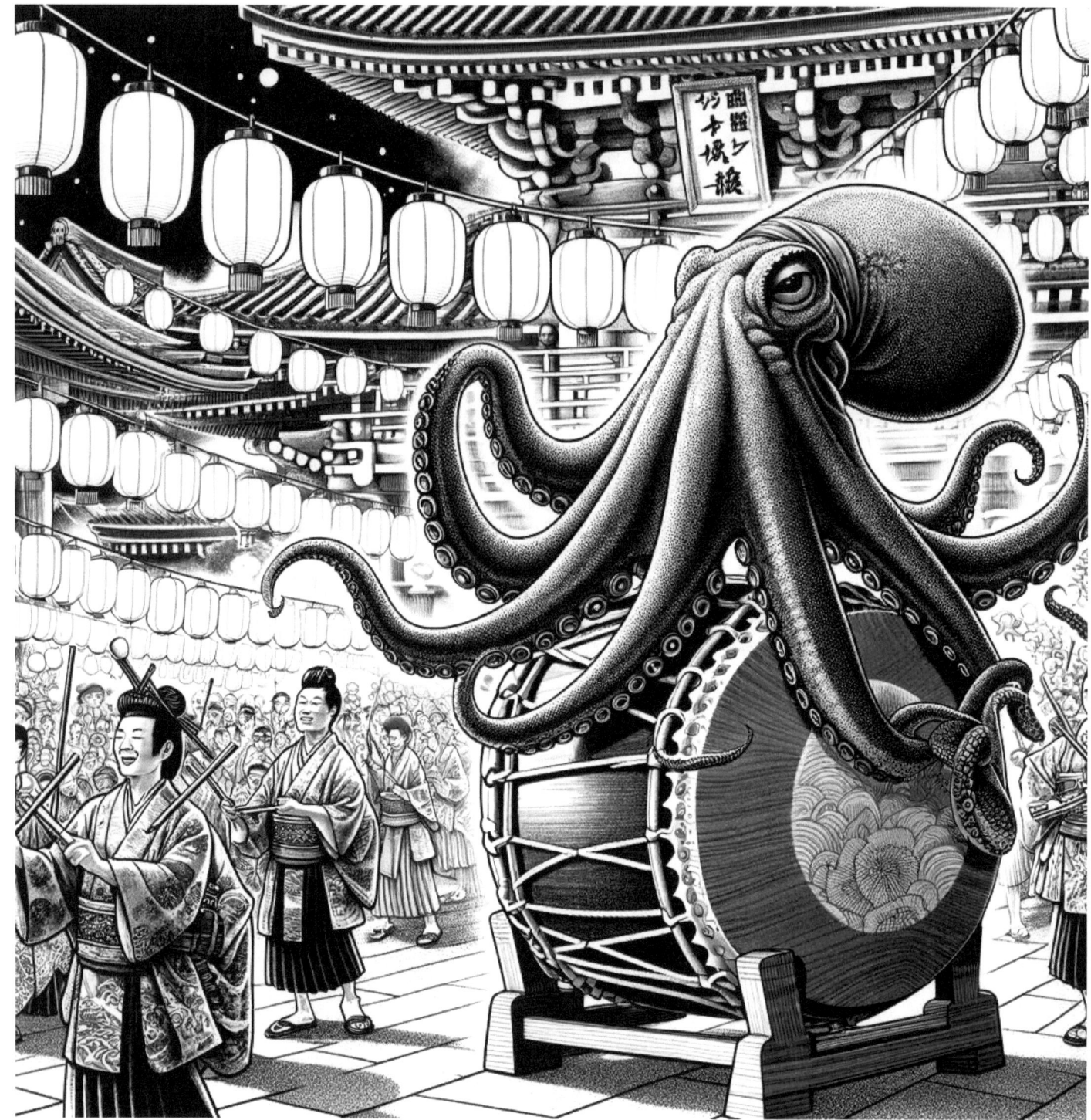

Figure 18. Volunteer filling in for the sick drummers

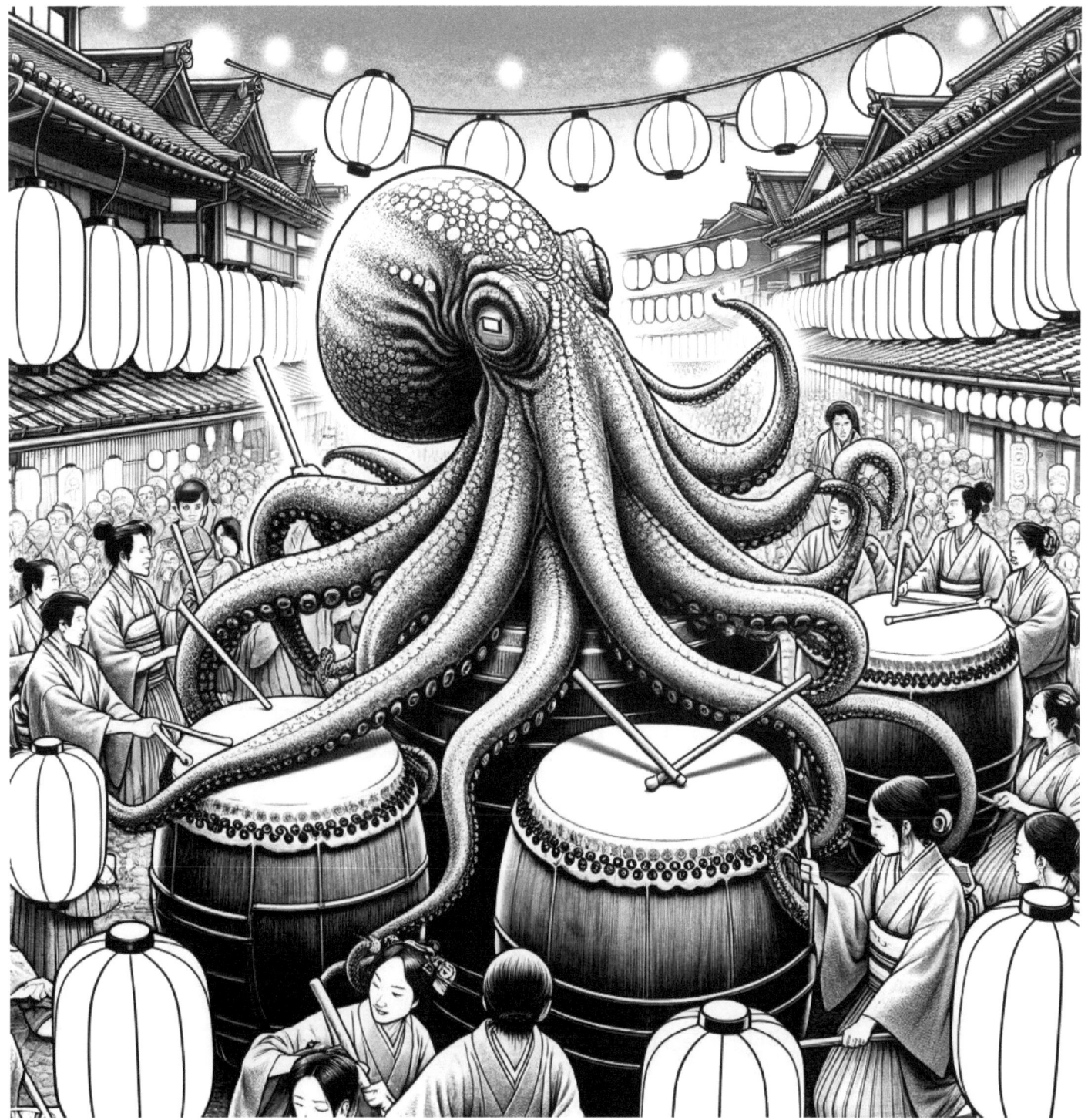

Figure 19. Since then, I've become part of the tradition...octaikopus! All this dedication has caused me to grow a few more legs...

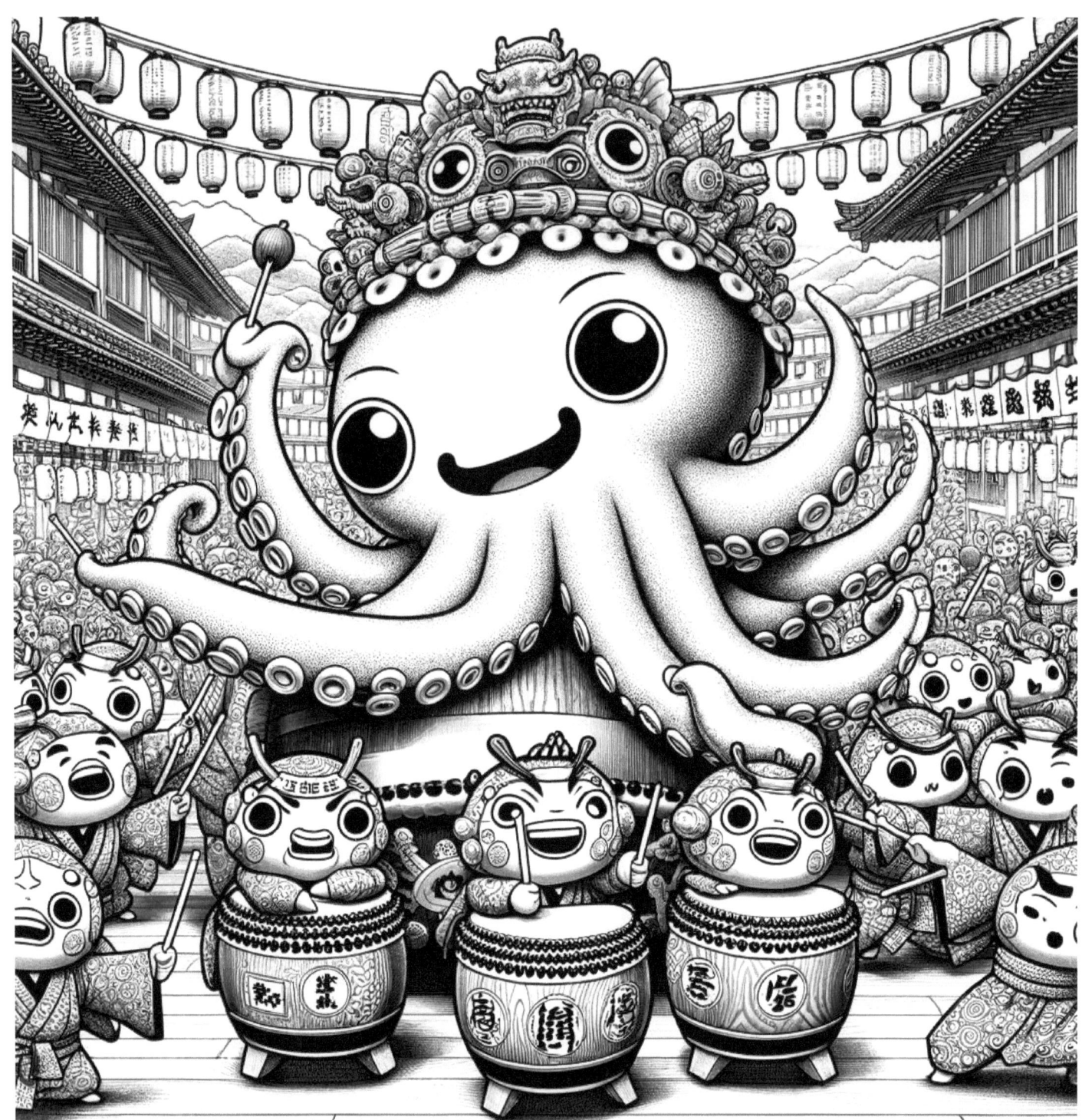

Figure 20. My kid too!

Worlds Collide

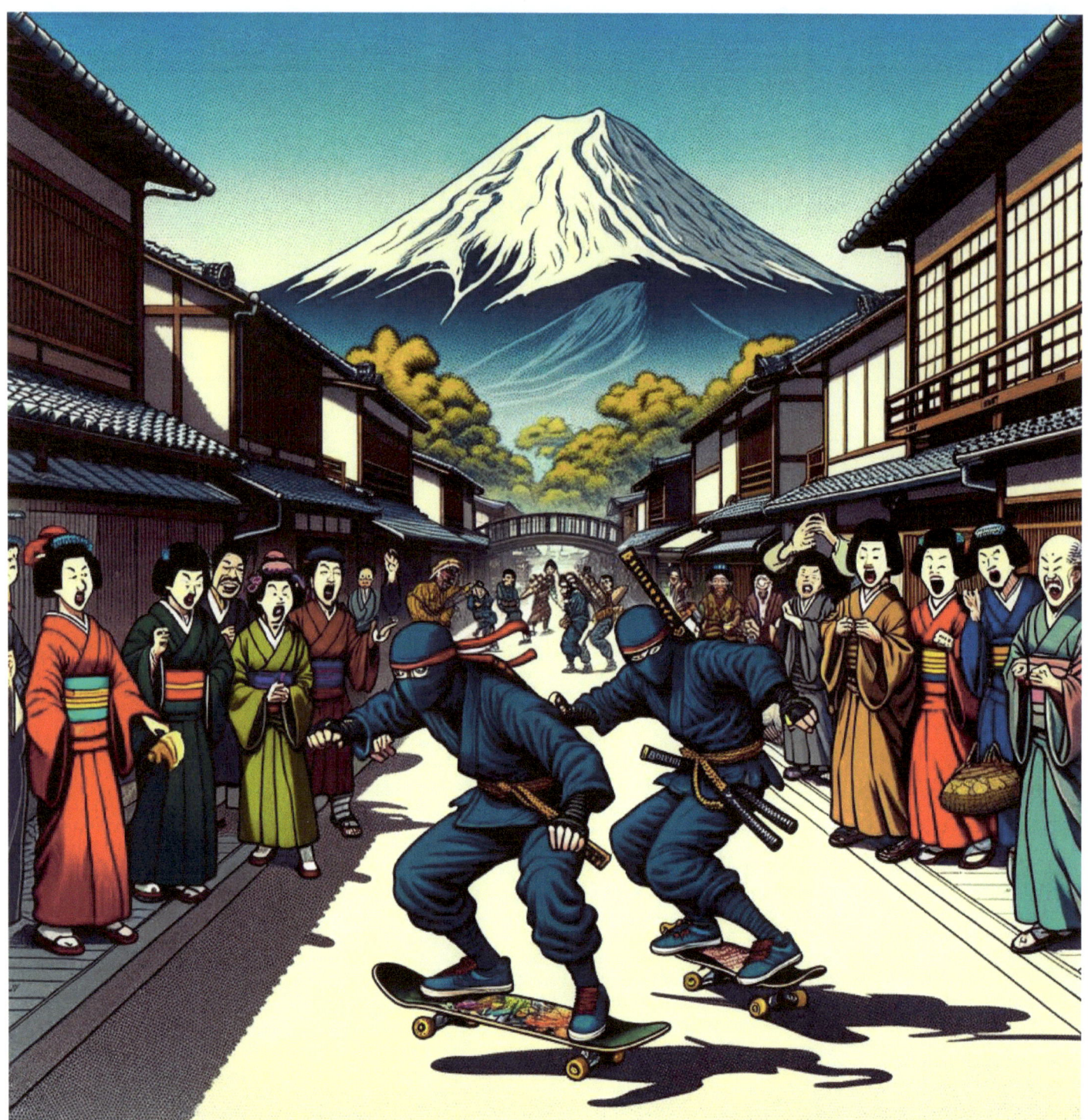

Figure 21. Cool kids of the 1700's

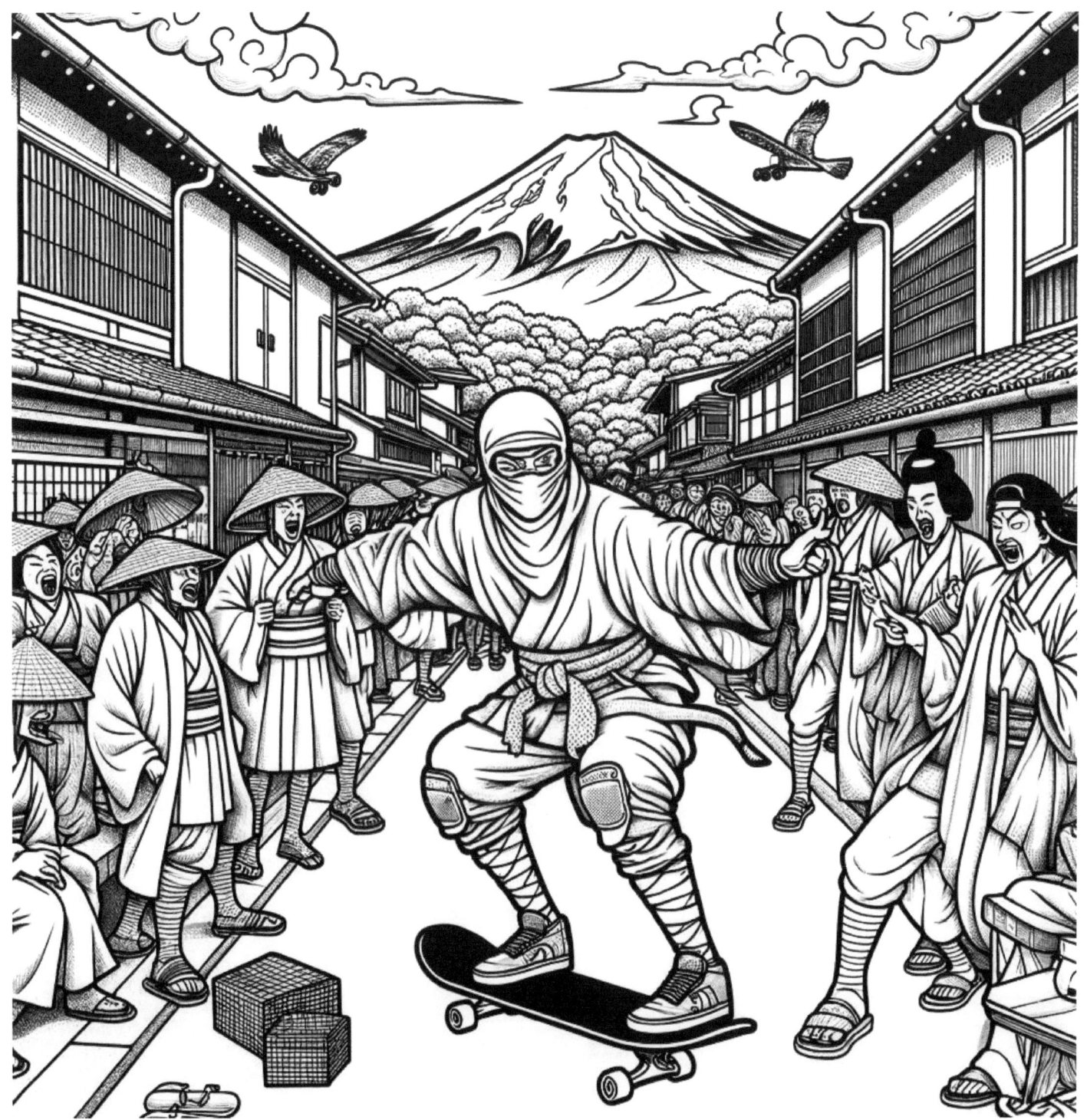

Figure 22. Hey quit laughing! Bystander: No self-respecting ninja wears kneepads!

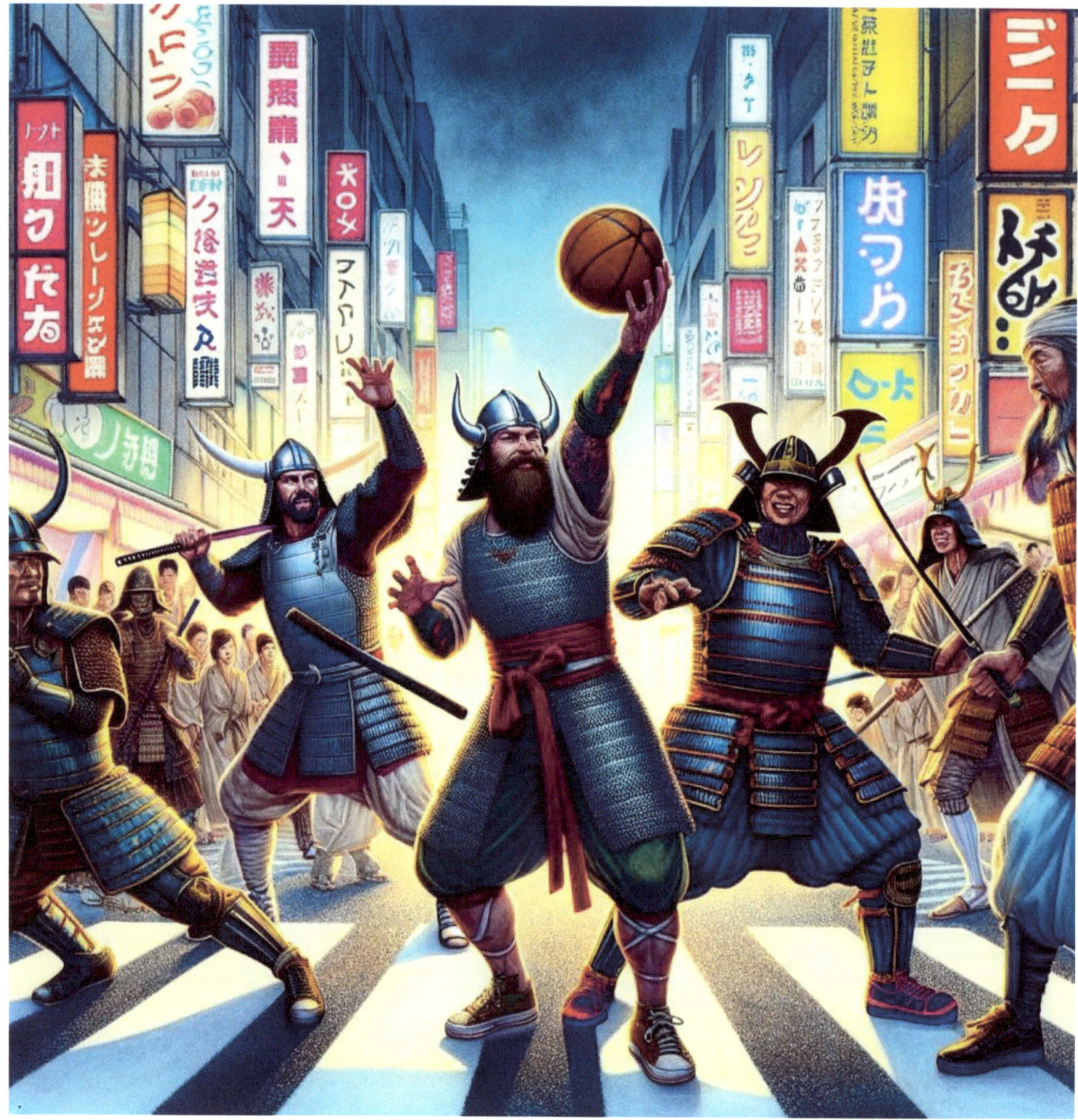

Figure 23. Summoning the power of Odin! We have arrived from the past to fulfill our destinies...Norway vs Japan in the streets of Tokyo!

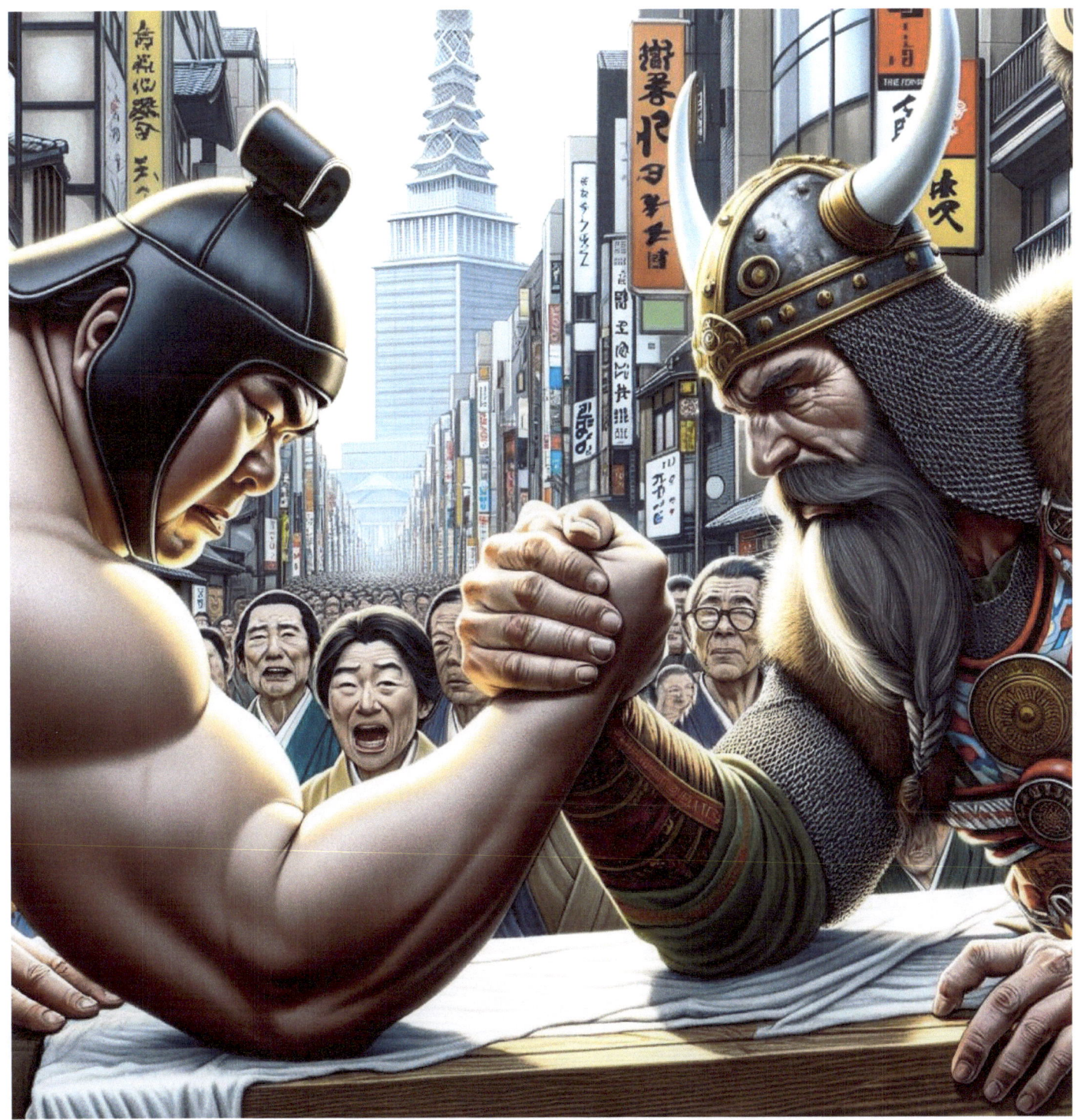

Figure 24. Final match...the honor of Japan is at stake! 90's trivia time: Reminds you of which game's cover art? Hint: It's an RTS...

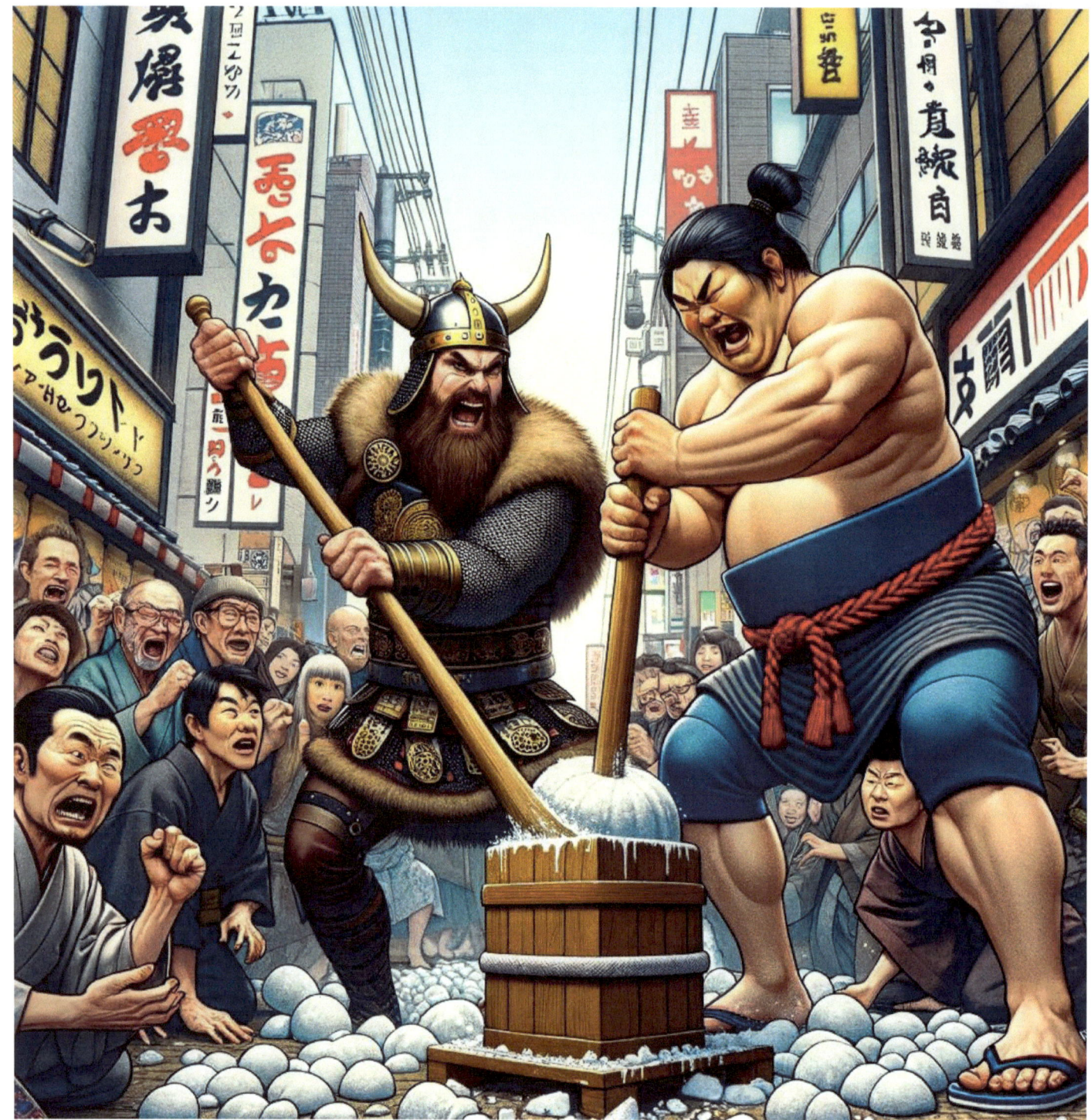

Figure 25. Let's unwind with the peaceful Japanese tradition of pounding mochi...the warrior spirit never dies!

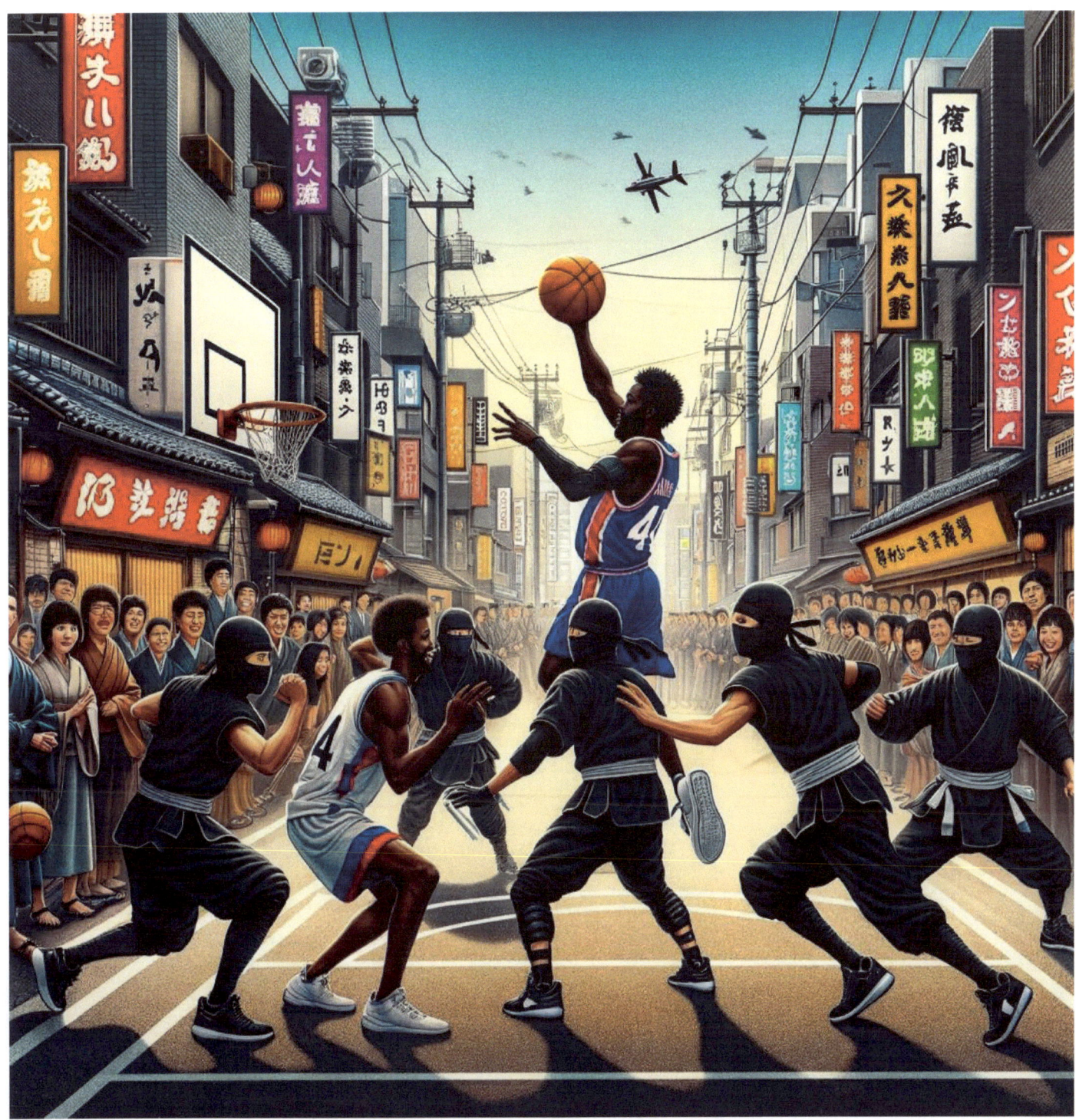

Figure 26. We got skillz...I know you got skillz too...

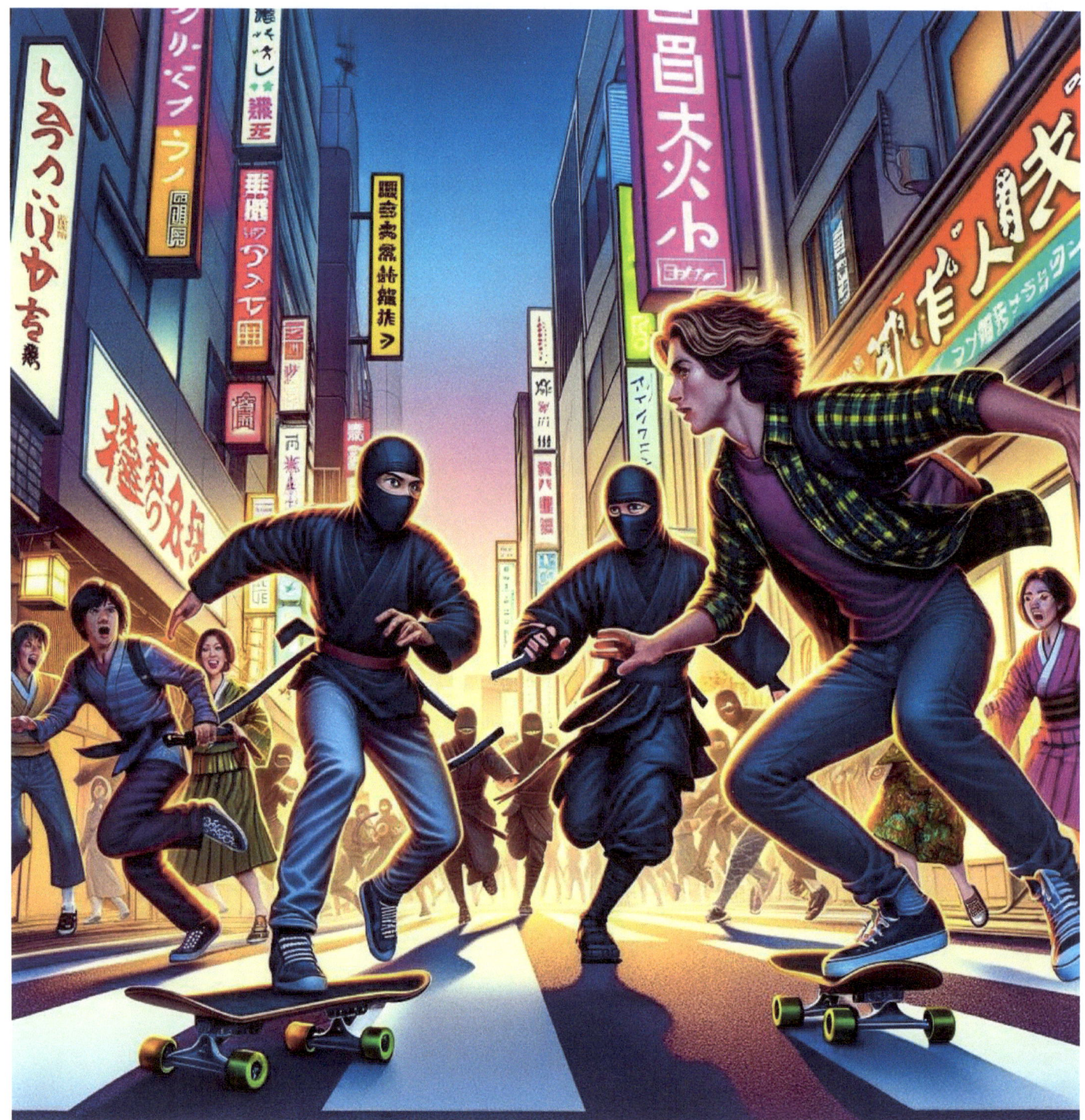

Figure 27. *Hey kid, you think you're too cool for us huh?*

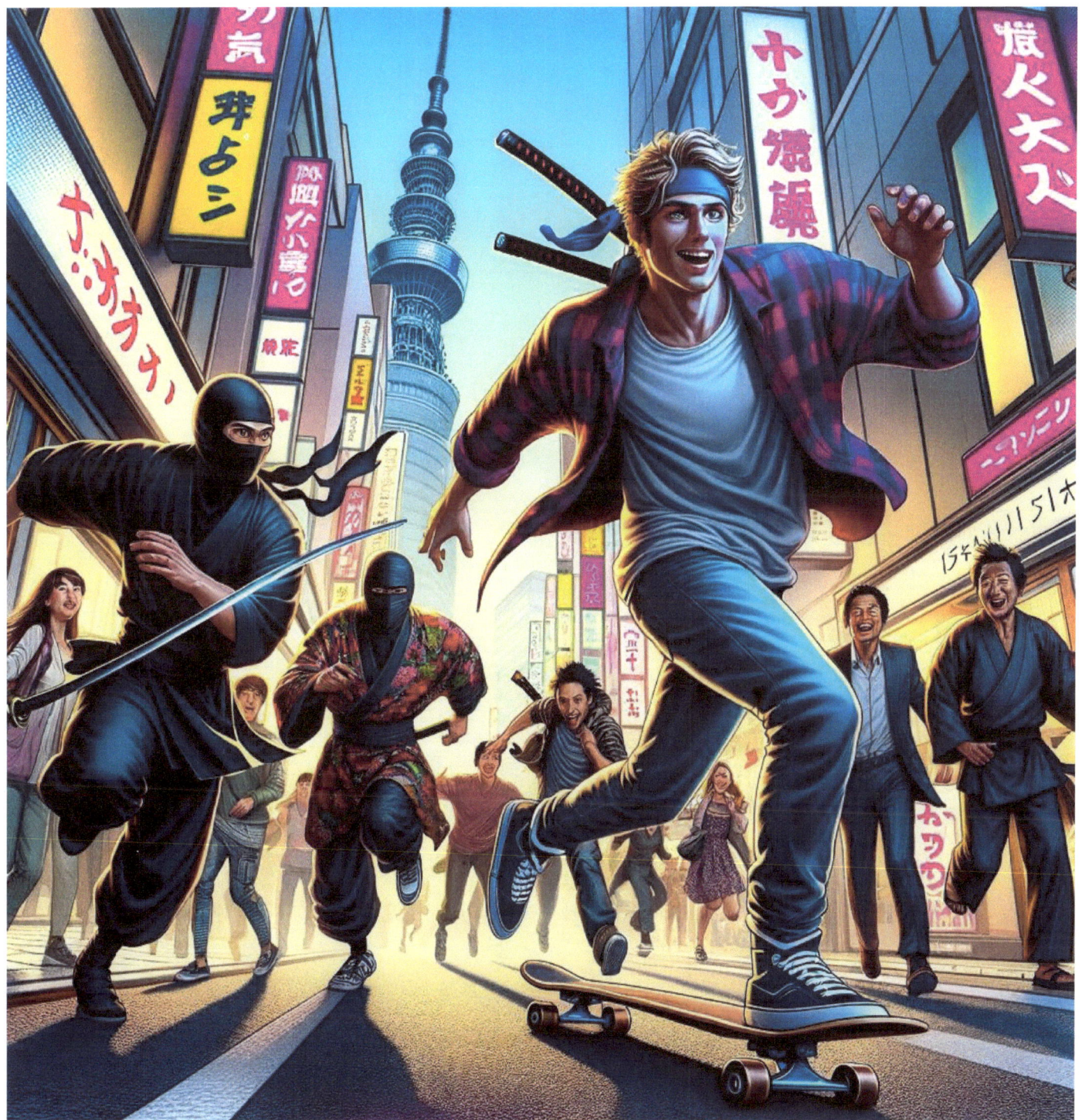

Figure 28. Hey, you're not allowed to carry those!

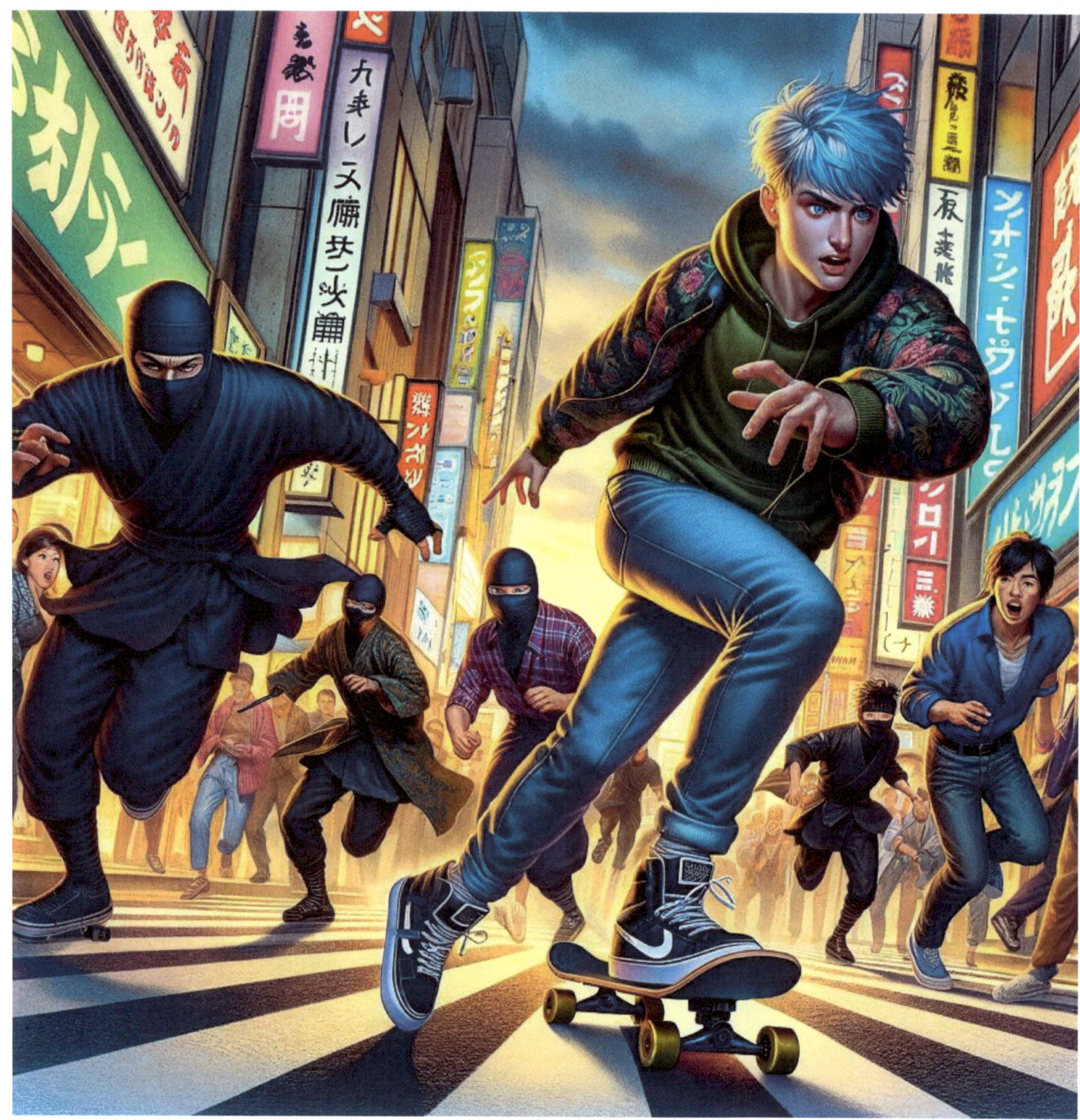

Figure 29. Oh crap, the Japanese undercover cops!

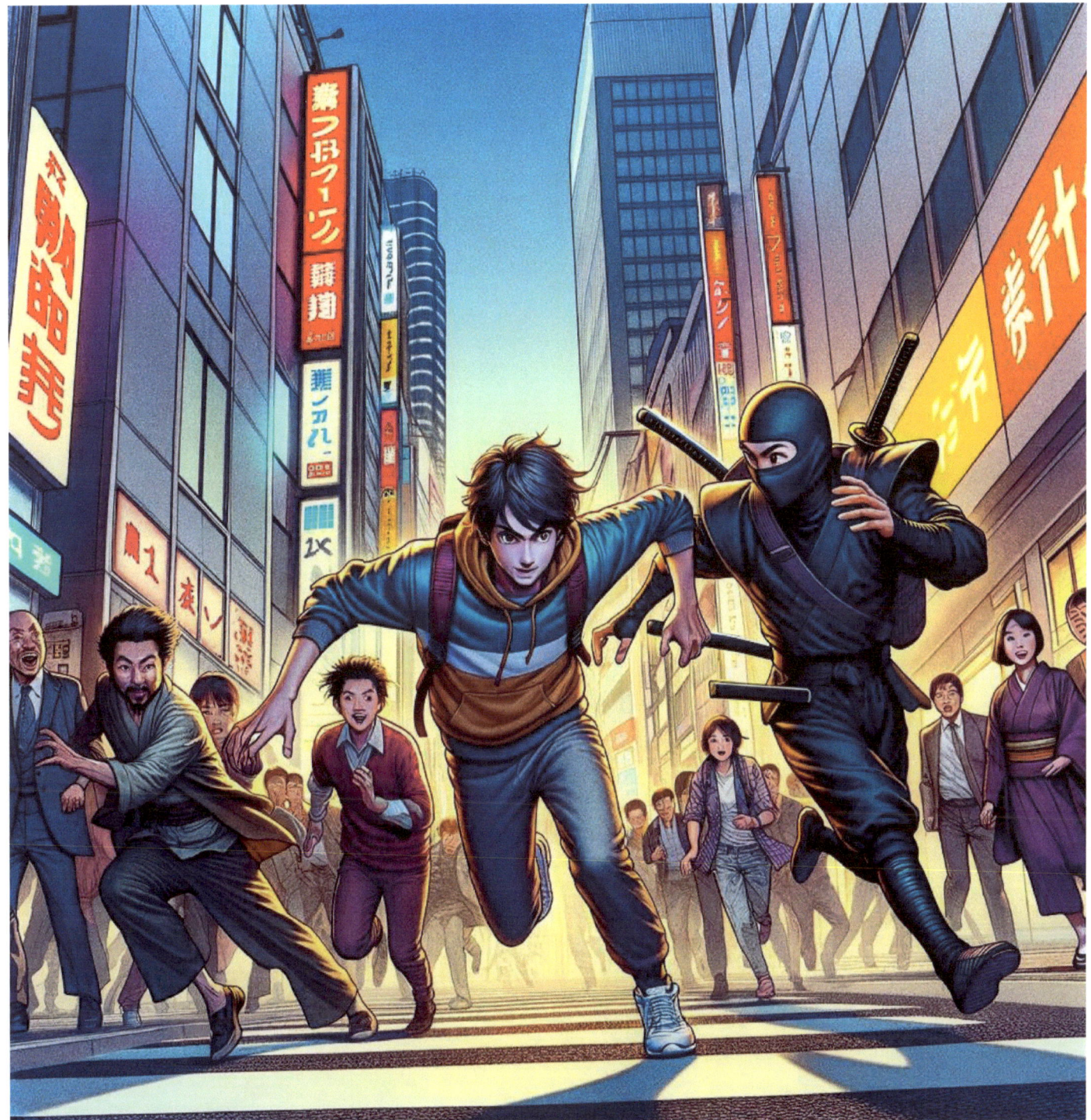

Figure 30. You think you can sprint kid?

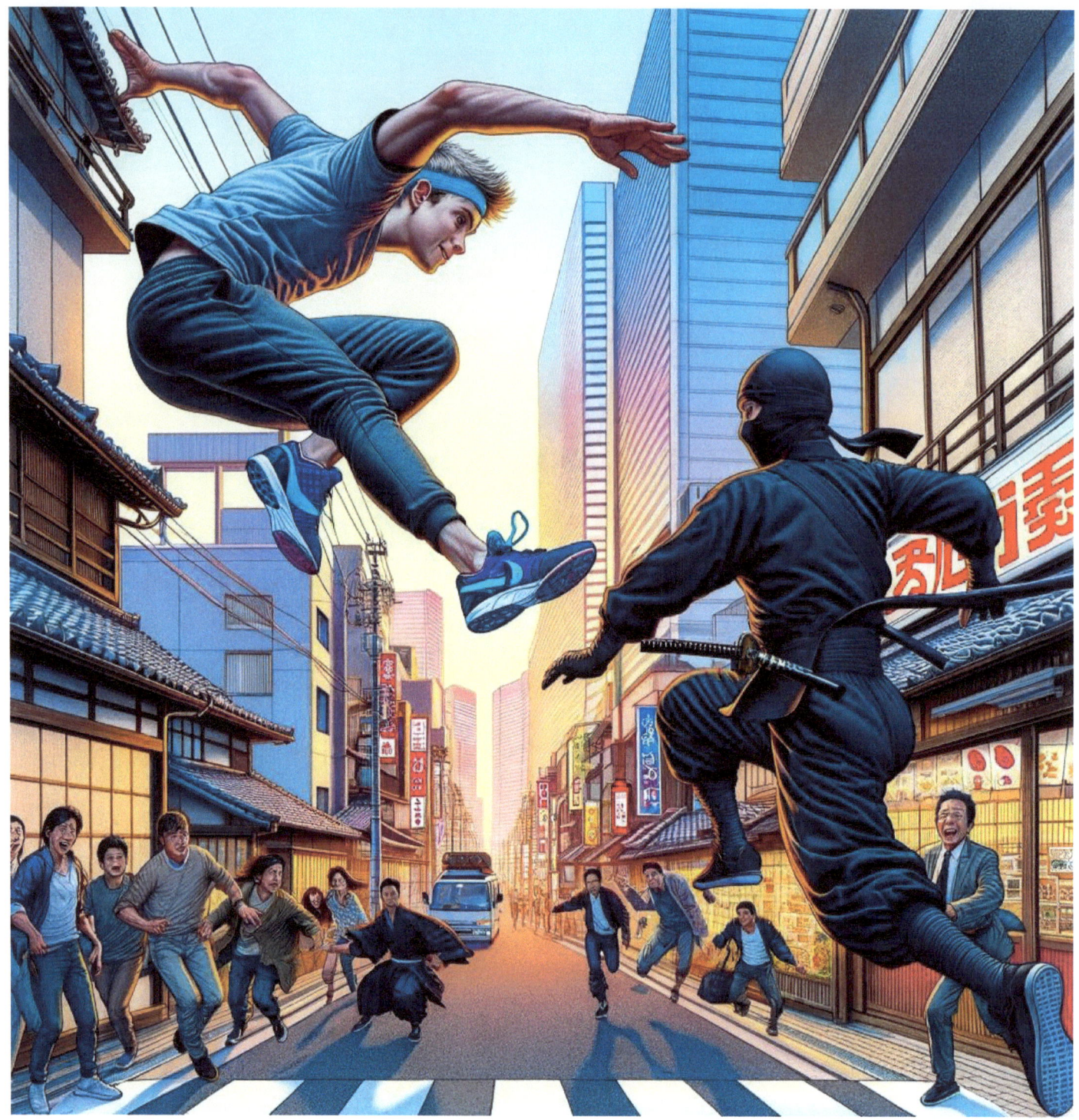

Figure 31. Nowhere to run, nowhere to hide...here goes

Black and White Copies - For Coloring

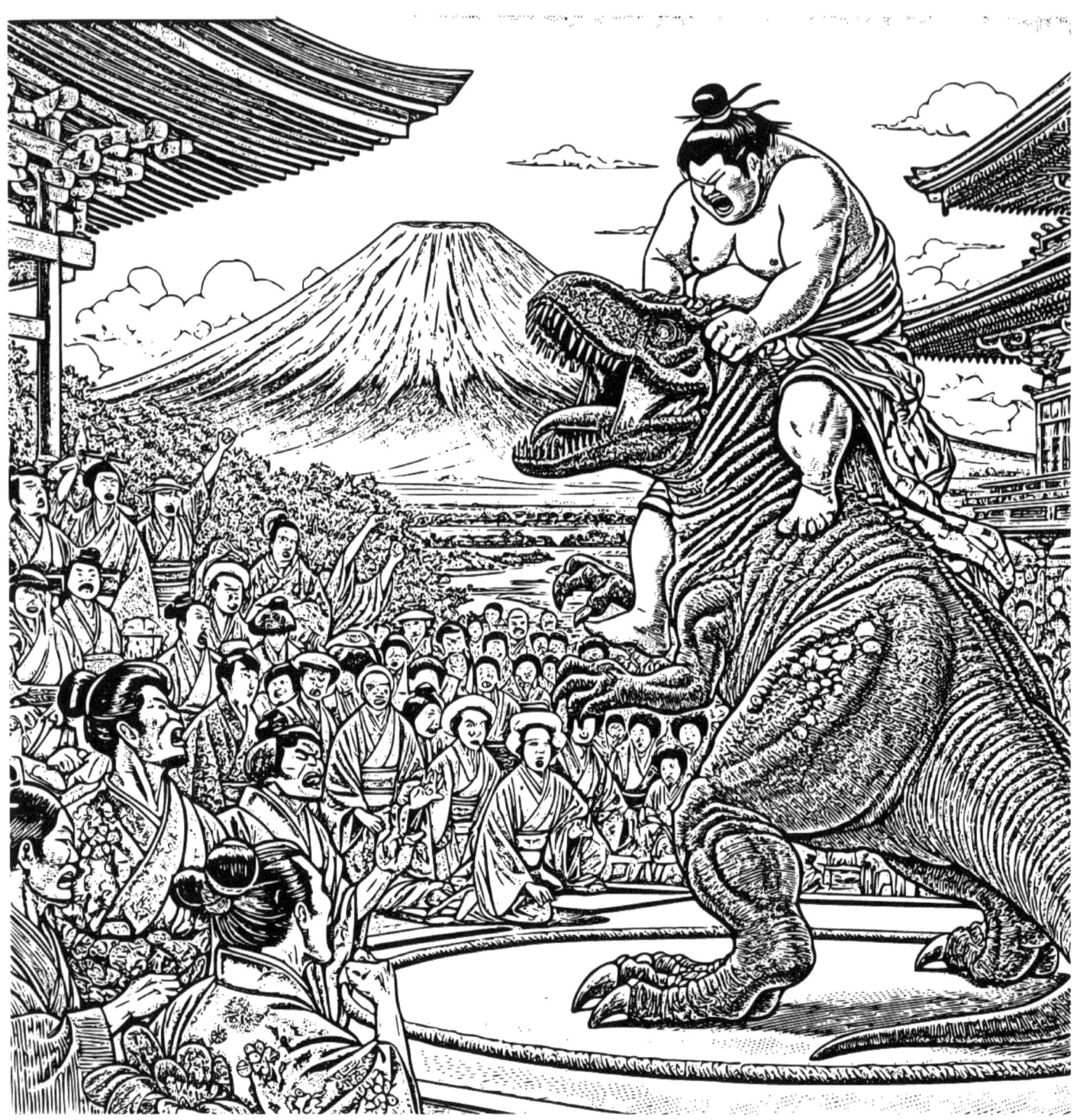

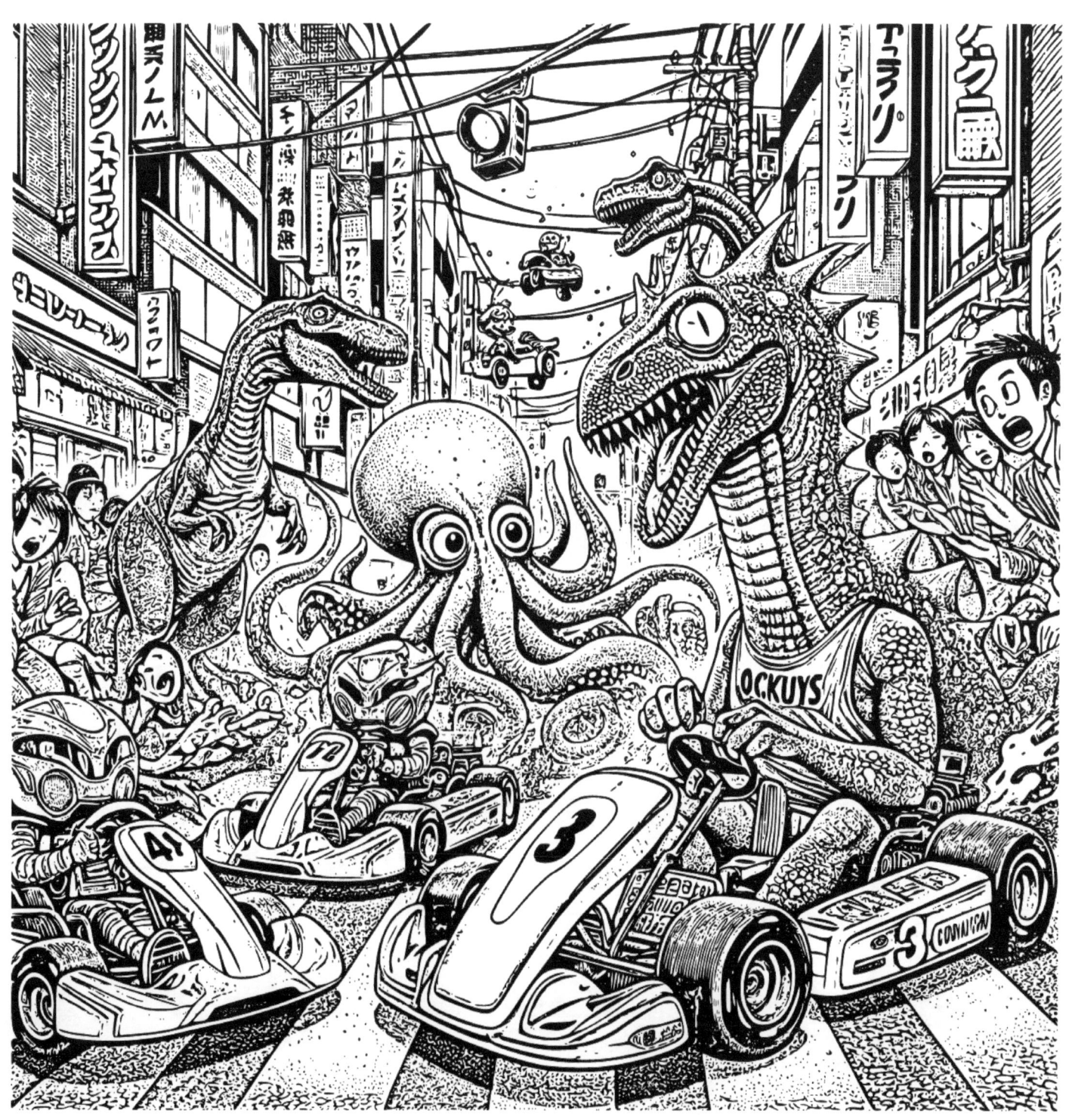

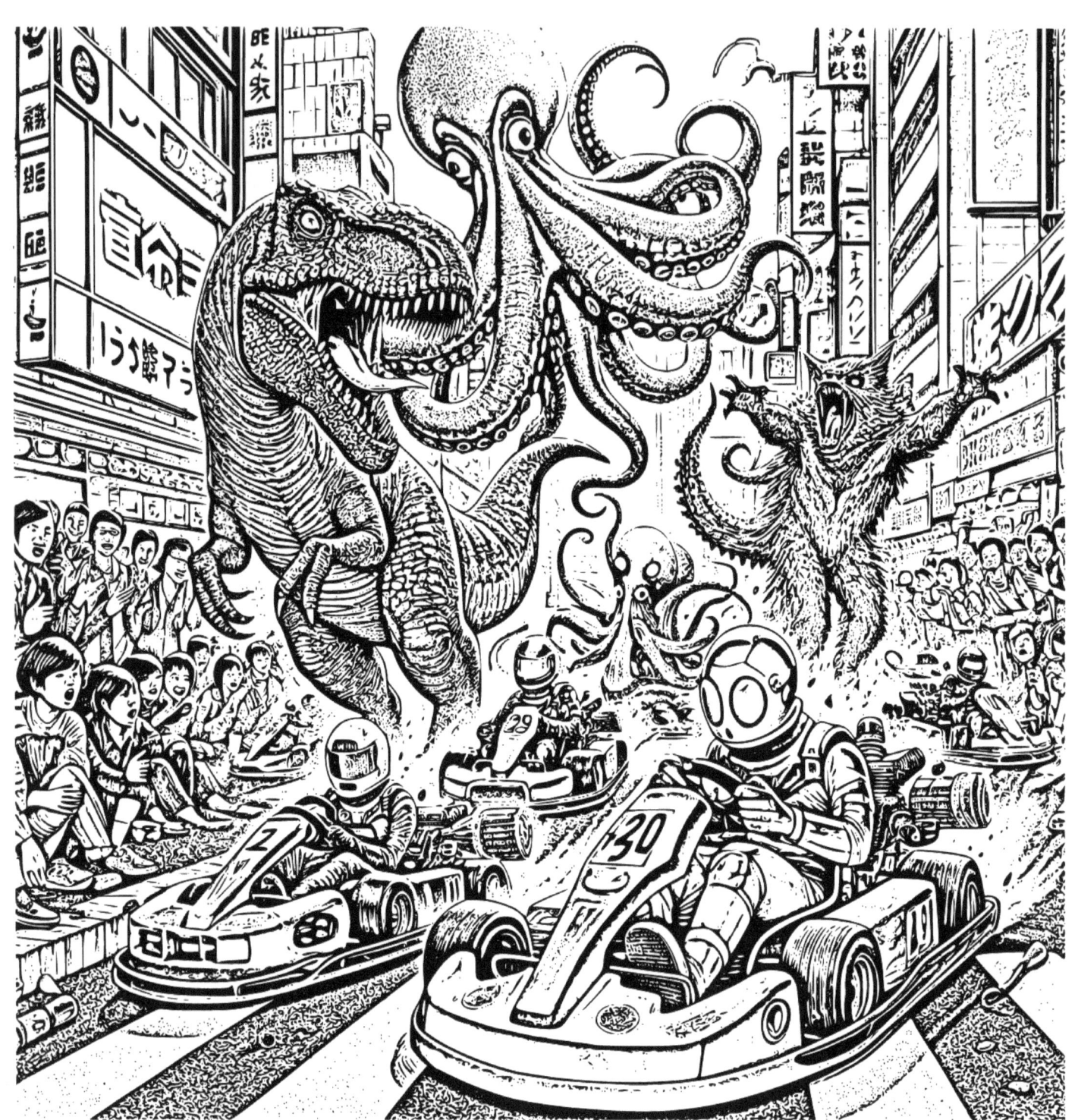

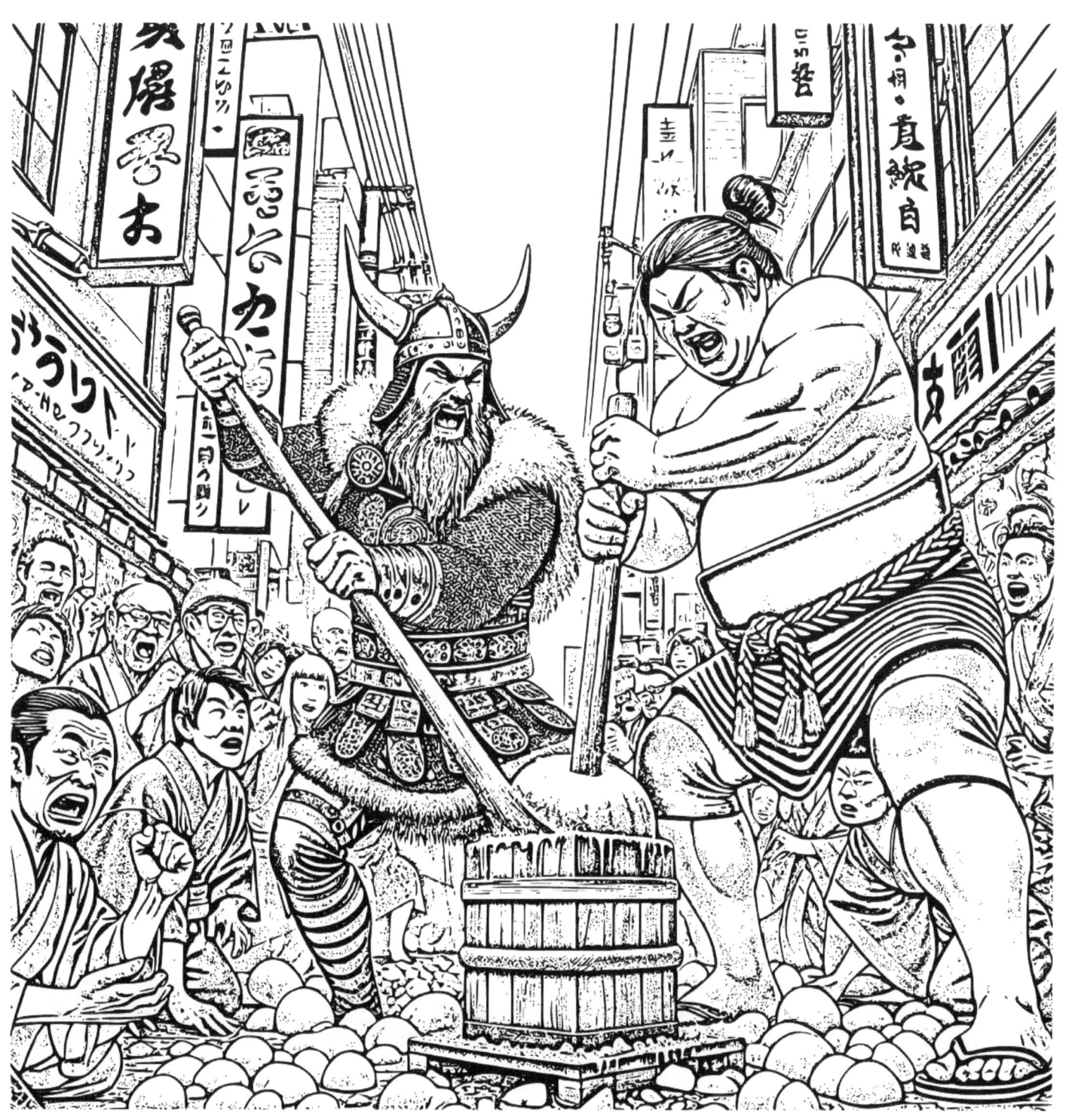

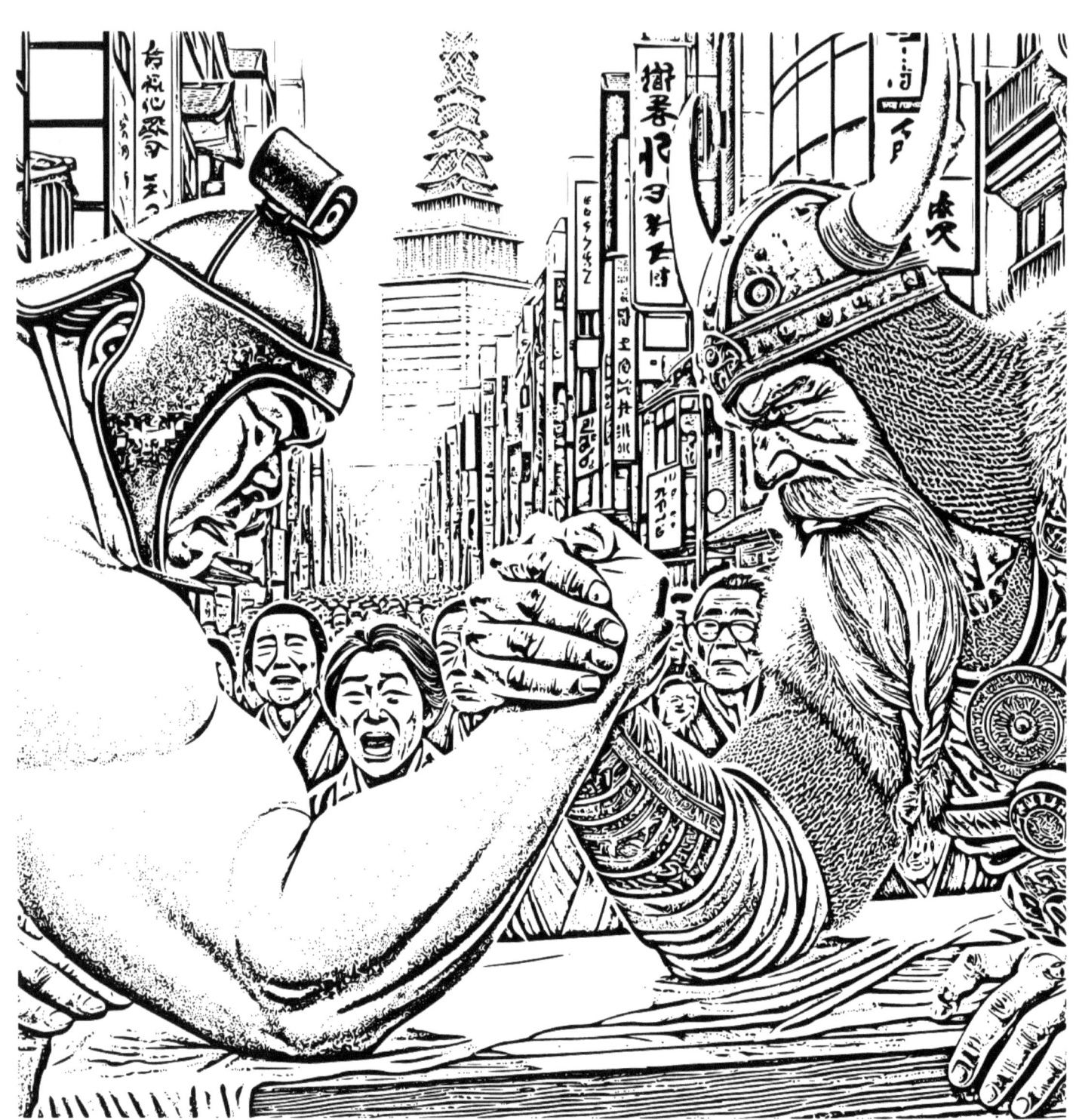

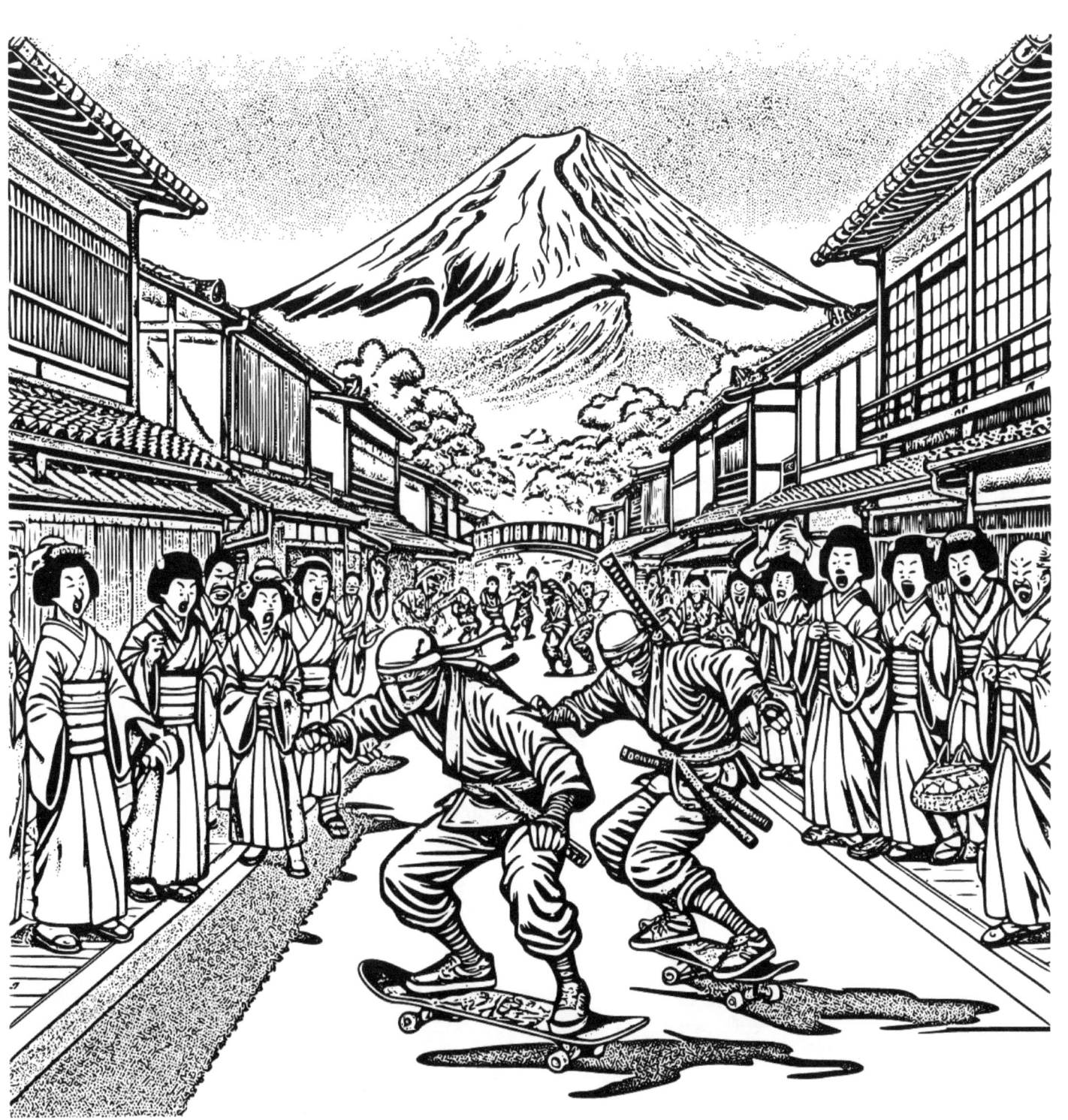

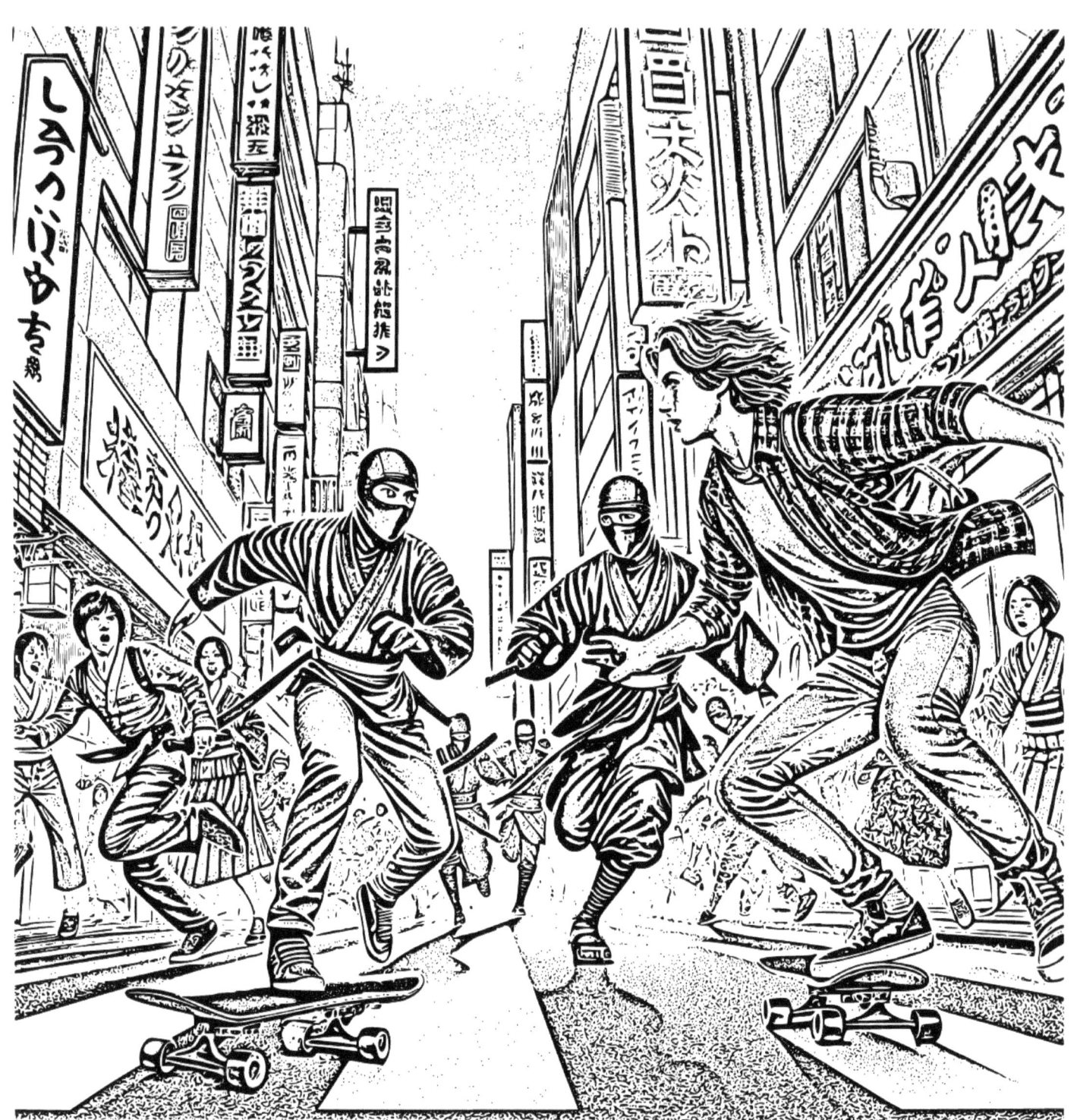

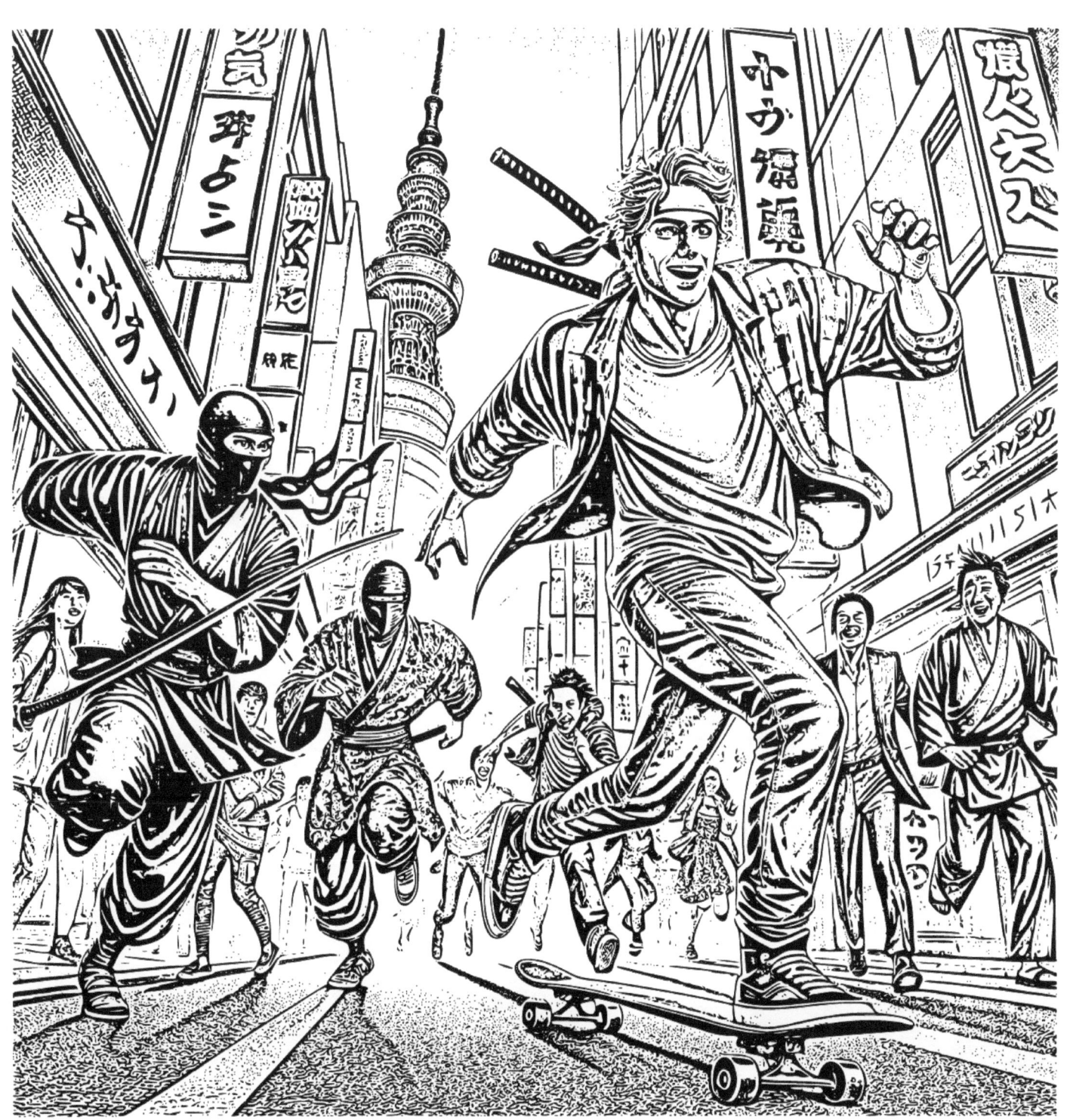

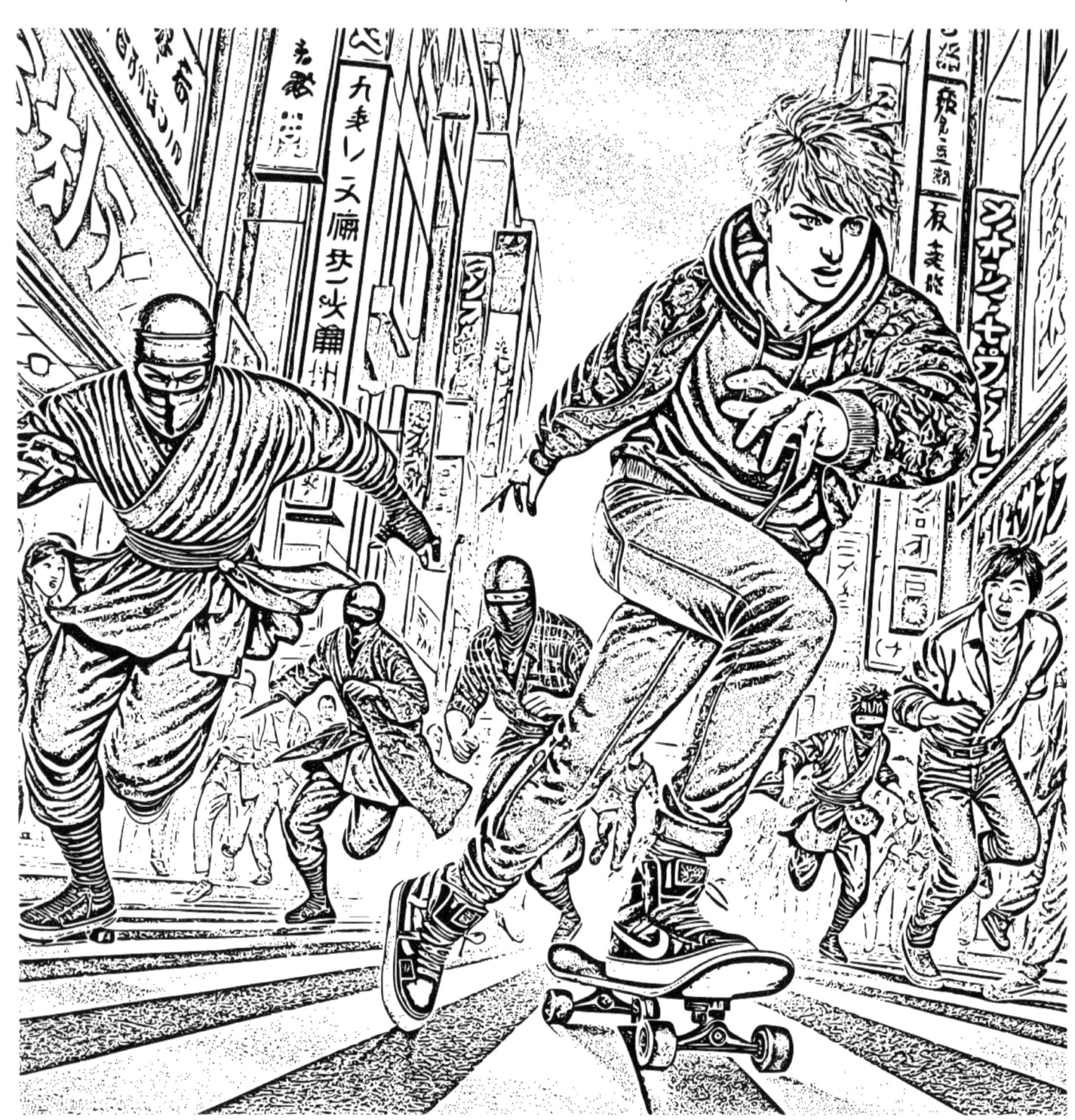

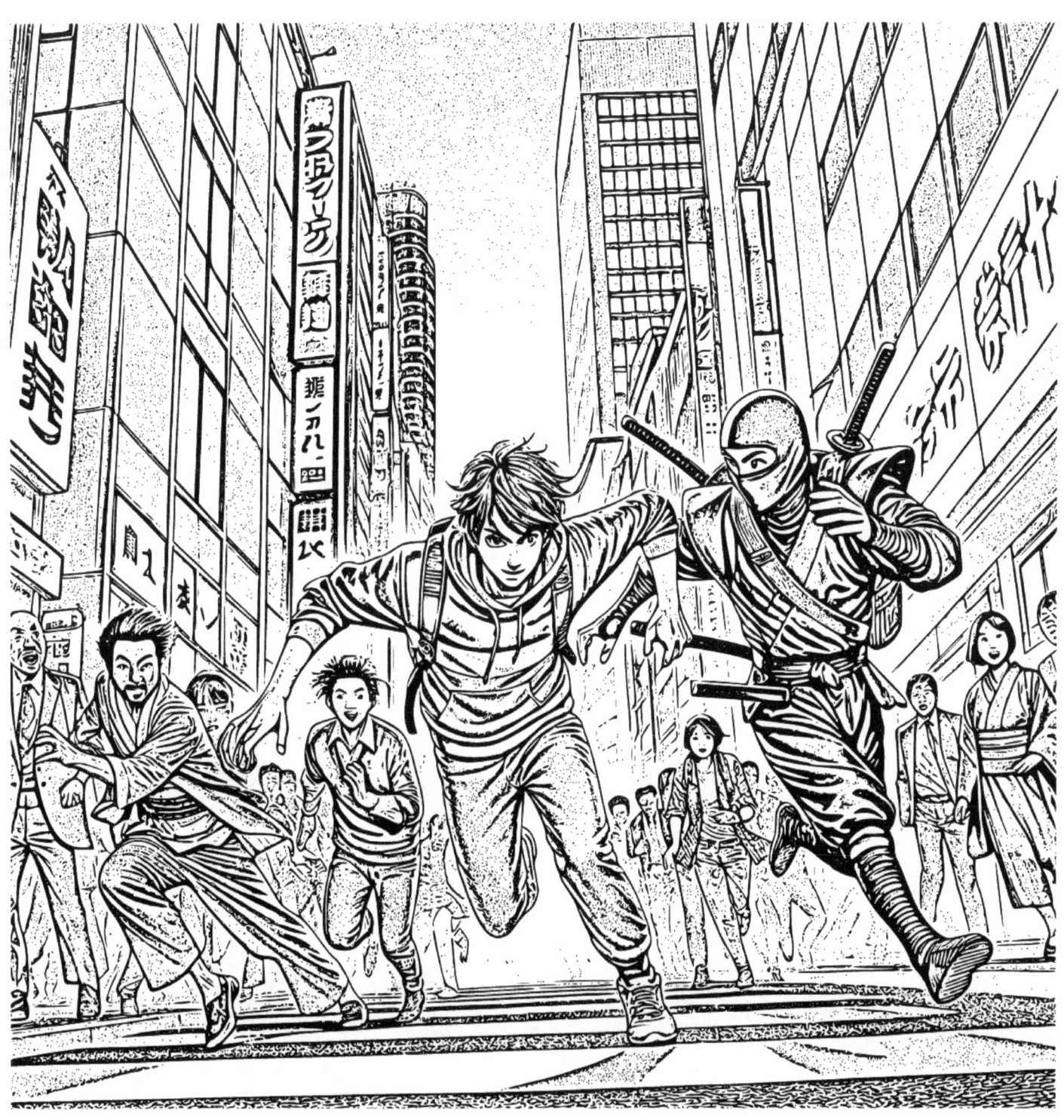

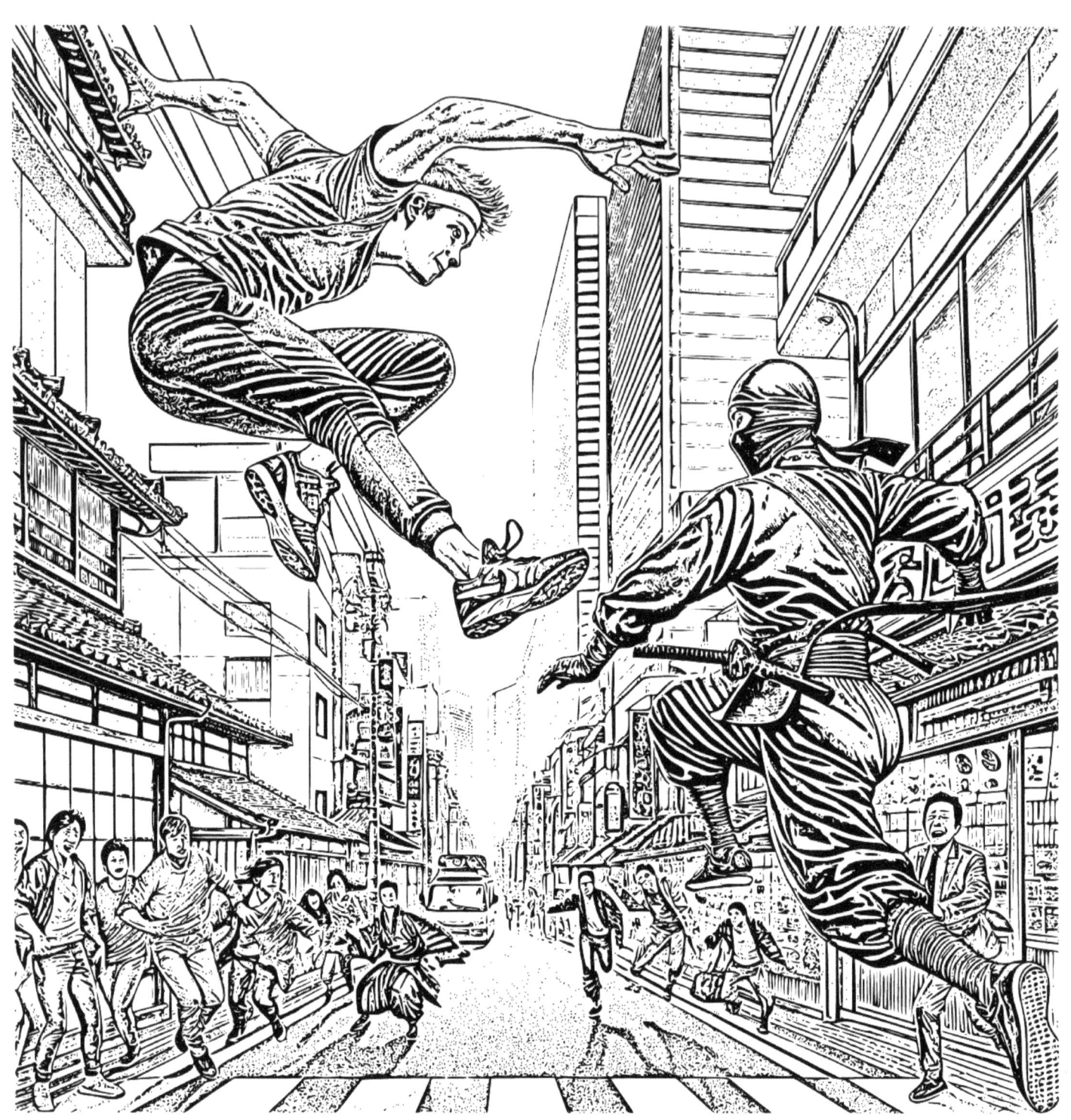